Barbara A. Shailor

THE MEDIEVAL BOOK

Illustrated from the Beinecke Rare Book
and Manuscript Library

Published by University of Toronto Press
Toronto Buffalo London
in association with the Medieval Academy of America

Medieval Academy Reprints for Teaching 28

*Z
6621
.B48
1991*

FRANKLIN PIERCE COLLEGE LIBRARY

© Medieval Academy of America 1991
Printed in United States of America
ISBN 0-8020-5910-4 (cloth)
ISBN 0-8020-6853-7 (paper)

First published by the Beinecke Rare Book and Manuscript Library, Yale
University, 1988. This edition is reprinted by arrangement with the
Beinecke Rare Book and Manuscript Library, Yale University Library.

Canadian Cataloguing in Publication Data

Beinecke Rare Book and Manuscript Library
The medieval book

(Medieval Academy reprints for teaching; 28)
Catalogue of an exhibition held Aug. 15 – Oct. 31, 1988.
Reprint. Originally published: The medieval book:
catalogue of an exhibition at the Beinecke Rare
Book & Manuscript Library, Yale University.
New Haven, Conn.: The Library, 1988.
ISBN 0-8020-5910-4 (bound) ISBN 0-8020-6853-7 (pbk.)

1. Beinecke Rare Book and Manuscript Library –
Exhibitions. 2. Manuscripts, Medieval – Connecticut
– New Haven – Exhibitions. 3. Manuscripts,
Renaissance – Connecticut – New Haven – Exhibitions.
4. Bibliographical exhibitions – Connecticut –
New Haven. I. Shailor, Barbara A., 1948-   .
II. Medieval Academy of America. III. Title. IV. Series.

Z6621.B48 1991   011′.31′0747468   C91-094121-1

Introduction

The Medieval Book celebrates the Beinecke Rare Book and Manuscript Library's distinguished collection of manuscripts from the Middle Ages and the Renaissance. It is the fourth in a series of six exhibitions prepared in honor of the twenty-fifth anniversary of the library, each of them focusing on one of its important collections.

While there has been remarkable growth in the holdings of early manuscripts at Yale since the opening of the Beinecke Library in 1963, the history of the collection reaches back to the first decade of the university. The fifteenth-century copy of the *Speculum humanae salvationis* presented by Elihu Yale to the Collegiate School in Connecticut in 1714 is believed to be the first illuminated manuscript in an American college library. Although enthusiasm for rare books flourished at Yale in the eighteenth and nineteenth centuries, it was not until after the Second World War that a collection of medieval and Renaissance manuscripts began to take shape under the guidance of librarians and bibliophiles James T. Babb, Thomas E. Marston, and Herman W. Liebert. Outstanding acquisitions, such as the Capitularies of Charlemagne, the Albergati Bible, and the Rothschild Canticles, were made possible through the generosity and keen interest of Edwin J. Beinecke, who personally selected many of the volumes he presented to Yale. Today there are more than 680 items in the Beinecke Library's general collection of pre-1600 manuscripts, some 230 Marston manuscripts, and noteworthy early manuscripts in both the Osborn and Mellon Alchemical collections. In addition, the Beinecke Library has hundreds of fragments not catalogued individually.

The theme of this exhibition is the medieval book—its development, construction, and function in the Middle Ages and Renaissance. The exhibition and catalogue reflect recent, and sometimes controversial, developments in the interdisciplinary field of manuscript studies. For centuries philologists, linguists, and historians have read medieval books to study the language of a given work or to establish an accurate and readable text; art historians have considered illuminated manuscripts as important repositories for works of art. But since the 1950s new interest has developed in the overall physical format of the medieval book and its historical context—how manuscript books were made and how they have deepened our understanding of the intellectual and social milieu of the Middle Ages and Renaissance. While many prominent scholars remain passionately committed to the primacy of the text, they are increasingly challenged by colleagues who fervently advocate the study of medieval books not only as artistic and literary documents, but also as artifacts that increase our knowledge of the social and intellectual history of the period to which they belonged.

The richness of the early manuscript collections in the Beinecke Library has suggested two related approaches to the medieval book, both derived from this new wave of scholarship. The first series of items examines the manuscript book as an archeological artifact of a period when mass-production was unknown and every volume had to be written and assembled by hand. Selected details of physical format, script, decoration, and binding are discussed, as well as parchment, paper, and the various types of ornamental initials, borders, and miniatures that often made the medieval book a brilliant artistic achievement.

In the second part of the exhibition, books are grouped by genre—both religious and secular—to show how the contents of a volume and its function within society influenced its physical appearance and the way in which it was produced. Fashion, use, and financial considerations dictated the design of the book, the style of its script and illumination, and the manner in which it was bound. As a result, the medieval book appeared in a myriad of forms ranging from modestly executed monastic texts to lavishly illuminated Books of Hours popular with the wealthy laity of the fifteenth century. A brief look at the transition from manuscript to printed book concludes the survey.

This exhibition and catalogue are intended for the non-specialist, though the descriptions and photographic reproductions may also be of value to scholars, particularly those unfamiliar with the Beinecke Library's holdings. While few collections could document every feature of medieval book production or every genre of manuscript, we have tried to offer a useful overview. The selected bibliography at the end of the catalogue suggests further general readings on a variety of topics.

I am deeply indebted to friends and colleagues who have generously contributed their insights and expertise. Robert G. Babcock, Edwin J. Beinecke Curator of Early Books and Manuscripts, and Consuelo W. Dutschke commented on early drafts of the text and helped to eliminate errors of omission and oversimplification. Jane Greenfield selected materials for the section on binding, assisted in the physical presentation of the exhibition, and contributed all of the line drawings. Edward Brian Roots and James T. Powell diligently labored as my research assistants. Among the many scholars who shared information concerning specific manuscripts, I should like to thank Bernhard Bischoff, Walter Cahn, Albert Derolez, Dianne Creasy Durante, A. S. G. Edwards, Stephen Emmel, Mrs. John D. Gordan, Jr., Jeffrey Hamburger, George R. Keiser, Laura Light, Rosemarie P. McGerr, Albinia de la Mare, James Marrow, Richard H. Rouse, Kathleen L. Scott, M. Alison Stones, and Linda E. Voigts. Material for the exhibition was kindly lent by Alvin Eisenman, Jean Preston, the American Oriental Society, the Yale Law School, and the Medical Historical Library. I am grateful to the staff of the Beinecke Library, especially to the director, Ralph W. Franklin, who has enthusiastically supported my work on this project and others, and to Christa Sammons, curator of the German Literature collection, the editor of this catalogue.

The Medieval Book

PAPYRUS *For thousands of years literary texts and documents were written not on parchment or paper, the preferred materials of the Middle Ages, but on sheets produced from the fibrous stalks of the papyrus plant. Papyrus was the primary writing material for Greece and Rome, as well as for Egypt, where the plant flourished in the swamplands of the Nile. After thinly slicing the pithy stalk lengthwise and carefully arranging the narrow strips in vertical rows for a first layer and in horizontal rows for a second, the maker could prepare a flat though fibrous writing surface by pressing or pounding the two layers together, a natural glue-like substance in the stalk of the plant providing the adhesive to bind the strips. When the sheets had dried, the surface was burnished with a stone, shell, or smooth piece of ivory. The completed sheets were assembled into long rolls by overlapping their vertical edges and pasting the seams.*

Writing on Papyrus

I P.CtYBR inv. 8
Homer, *Iliad* 22.254–99,
350–55, 358–62, 364–65
Egypt, 1st or early 2nd century

Evidence from surviving papyrus fragments indicates that the early format for texts was not the codex, or book as we know it today, but the roll, inscribed and read horizontally from end to end. Beginning at the left-hand edge of a sheet of papyrus, the scribe copied the text in a column from the top to the bottom of the writing surface. Upon finishing one column, he moved to the right and began another, continuing column by column until the entire text had been copied. These papyrus fragments from the Faiyum region in Egypt date from the first or second century of the present era and record portions of Homer's *Iliad*. The reconstruction of the various pieces reveals that much of one column, together with parts of two subsequent columns, still remains intact. If, as was often the case, each papyrus roll contained a single book or unit of an author's work, then this roll would have consisted of fifteen columns approximately thirty-six lines long. The entire *Iliad* would have occupied nearly three hundred running feet of papyrus.

Papyrus Roll

2 P.CtYBR inv. 2753
Contents unknown
Egypt, date unknown

Because of the age and fragile nature of papyrus, most rolls made from the material are fragmentary. This papyrus roll, however, is in its original state, never having been opened. Presented to the library in 1972 by Thomas E. Marston, it is of unknown origin, though it probably derives from Egypt, the source of most extant papyri. A simple clay holder, stamped with the seals of its owner, protects the unidentified document within.

Papyrus Book

3 P.CtYBR inv. 1788
Apocryphal story about
Mary, mother of Jesus
(in Coptic)
Egypt, 9th? century

Even after codices replaced rolls as the primary format for texts during the late Roman Empire, papyrus continued to be a common writing material. This fragment of a Coptic manuscript book from the ninth century, for instance, is written on papyrus, its two extant leaves preserving part of a legend about Mary. The sewing holes of the original binding are visible in the center of the two pages indicating that the text was read in the form of a book, rather than as a roll.

2 *Papyrus roll with seal intact.*

3 *Fragment of a papyrus book with sewing holes.*

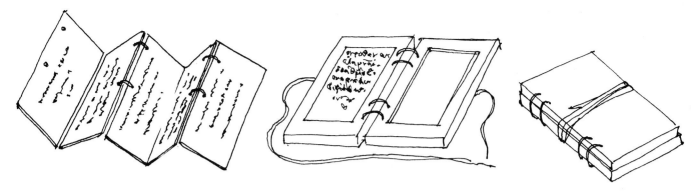

Wooden tablets.

The origins of the medieval codex can be traced to the classical practice of writing on ivory or wooden tablets. Some tablets had a hollowed out area filled with wax, onto which the writer would scratch accounts or rough drafts with a sharp instrument; later, if the text were no longer of interest, the wax could be smoothed over and made ready to receive more notes. Other wooden tablets, such as those discovered at Vindolanda in northern England, were written on directly with pen and ink. Several tablets of either format could easily be linked with strips of leather, hemp, or linen, or with metal rings; the linked tablets could then be folded and secured with a thong. In some cases two wax-surfaced tablets were joined to form a diptych, so that the text on the inner surface was concealed and protected when the tablets were closed. The term *codex*, by which the Romans meant two or more writing tablets linked together, is generally used today to refer to the medieval manuscript book of this shape. Practical considerations and historical changes during the Christian era contributed to the increased popularity of the codex over the roll. A codex is far more convenient to use, presenting fewer storage problems and eliminating the tedious task of rerolling. Christians apparently adopted the manuscript codex early in the second century: when the Christian Bible began to circulate, it was copied on papyrus but in codex form. The early Christians may have embraced this format to distinguish their texts from those of Judaism and paganism, which were written in rolls. By the beginning of the fourth century, the codex became the predominant medium for both Christian and non-Christian literature, and the use of the roll sharply diminished.

PARCHMENT AND PAPER *Although books produced in Egypt continued to be composed of papyrus leaves well into the tenth and eleventh centuries, parchment made from animal skins was the common material, or what is technically called the support, for the book in the early Middle Ages. Parchment surpassed papyrus in importance during the Middle Ages for several reasons. More durable in humid climates, it was better suited for the long-term preservation of business records and literary texts. Well-prepared parchment offered a smoother surface for the scribe and decorator on both sides of a leaf. Erasures and corrections could be made on parchment without significantly weakening the support, whereas this was difficult to do on papyrus.*

The terms parchment and vellum are often used interchangeably, though precisely speaking, parchment is made from sheep, goat, or other animal skin, while vellum is unsplit calfskin. Specialized knowledge and a microscope are necessary to distinguish the two. Here the term parchment is used generically to refer to the writing support made from animal skins. The manufacture of parchment varied according to geographical area and specific time period, although certain details were similar. The pelt of the animal was soaked in a lime bath, dried while being stretched on a frame, and then cleaned and scraped. It is the process of simultaneously stretching and drying the pelt that distinguishes parchment from leather. Fine parchment was pumiced and chalked to milky white smoothness.

Parchment

The quality of the parchment depended upon both the age and type of animal skin and the care with which it was prepared; the skin of an unborn calf was especially prized for deluxe manuscripts. This Wycliffite New Testament produced in England around 1400 is written on parchment that retains many of the characteristic features of an animal pelt. The hair side is fuzzy or velvety to the touch and the hair follicles are clearly distinguishable; the texture is rough and the color somewhat mottled. An imperfection in the skin of the animal is visible in the lower margin of the leaf displayed.

4 Beinecke MS 125
Wycliffite New Testament (incomplete)
England, late 14th or early 15th century

This thick, coarse parchment contrasts with that used for Beinecke MS 407, a lavishly decorated Bible produced in Italy during the second quarter of the fifteenth century for Cardinal Niccolò Albergati. This parchment is so fine that it is virtually impossible to distinguish the hair side from the flesh side; each page is supple, unblemished, and uniformly white.

5 Beinecke MS 407
Latin Bible ("Albergati Bible")
Italy, 1428

Palimpsest

The strength and versatility of parchment are demonstrated by its re-use in palimpsests. If the contents of a parchment manuscript were no longer of value to the owner, the scribe could scrape or wash the ink off the skin and copy other texts onto the same leaves. Beinecke MS 262 consists almost exclusively of palimpsest leaves. The superimposed material, Greek liturgical texts, was probably copied in Italy during the fifteenth century by a clumsy scribe who frequently confused Greek and Italian. The many peculiarities of the language and the idiosyncratic addition of Greek accents suggest that the scribe had a tenuous understanding of Greek and may have been copying the text through dictation. Barely visible, though partially legible under ultraviolet light, is another text that was effaced to make room for the new one. To judge from its script, the older text was copied during the tenth century.

6 Beinecke MS 262
Liturgy (in Greek)
Italy, 15th century
(lower text: Saint's life, 10th century)

Binding Stays

A more humble use for parchment in medieval book production also deserves attention. In paper manuscripts of the fifteenth century parchment binding stays were commonly inserted throughout the manuscript to reinforce the paper at the points of sewing for the binding, a practice that can be traced back to early papyrus codices. A monastic binder would use bits and pieces of old parchment codices that were no longer of value to the monastery, outdated liturgical works being a prime source of scrap. Beinecke MS 225, which was probably bound in the Carthusian monastery at Erfurt in 1442 or shortly thereafter, has reinforcements from such a liturgical manuscript, written in the first half of the twelfth century. It is likely that other fifteenth-century manuscripts from this monastery would have parchment binding stays cut from the same liturgical manuscript.

7 Beinecke MS 225
Scholar's notebook on various philosophical works, largely Aristotelian
Bohemia, 1422

4 *Flesh side of parchment. MS 125, f. 14r.*

Hair side of the same leaf. MS 125, f. 14v.

6 *Palimpsest photographed under ultra-violet light. MS 262.*

Parchment, though an ideal material for the production of manuscript books, was an expensive commodity; a large codex might require as many as two hundred animal skins. Paper became an alternative to parchment as soon as it began to be made in quantity in Spain in the middle of the twelfth century. The use of paper gradually spread throughout the rest of western Europe until, in the second half of the fifteenth century, it contributed to the revolutionary change from manuscript to printed book. Early paper differs remarkably from most paper today: it was hand-produced from cloth rags and was low in acidity with long fibers. Beinecke MS 275, one of the earliest extant copies of the autobiography of the Jewish historian Josephus, was transcribed on paper in Byzantium at the end of the twelfth century or beginning of the thirteenth. The surface is rough and the color uneven as is often the case with paper of this period from the Near East.

Methods of production steadily improved, and by the fifteenth century fine paper was available both for plain text manuscripts and for those with elaborate decoration. Beinecke MS 226 is an excellent example of an attractively illuminated codex composed of both paper and parchment. Produced in Flanders in 1476, the manuscript contains a French translation of Caesar's *Gallic Wars* that was copied for a counselor of Charles the Bold of Burgundy. Though the paper appears thick by modern

Paper

8 Beinecke MS 275

Josephus, *Vita* (in Greek)

Byzantium, late 12th or early 13th century

9 Beinecke MS 226

Caesar, *Commentarii de bello gallico*, French tr. Jean Duchesne

Flanders, 1476

standards, there is a noticeable improvement in overall quality. The juxtaposition of paper with parchment is also significant: parchment leaves were inserted wherever an illuminated miniature was to appear in the text because parchment was a better surface than paper for applying gold leaf and paint. In general, however, fifteenth-century paper had certain advantages over parchment: it was easier to insure uniformity of color and texture, and it was easier to cut and fold paper sheets to the appropriate size.

Hand-produced paper was manufactured by placing the sun-dried and beaten pulp of fermented cloth rags in water and then scooping the fibers up into screen trays called paper molds. The mold consisted of a series of closely aligned parallel wires called laid lines arranged lengthwise in the tray; perpendicular to them, but at wider intervals, was another set of wires called chains. In the midst of this grid pattern was stitched a watermark design, also made of wire. The water from the pulp would seep through the screen tray; the paper that remained was dried first in a press between pieces of felt and then in the open air. The surface of the finished paper sheets was sized with gelatin or a comparable substance to prevent the ink from bleeding.

No two early molds for paper were exactly alike. The distance between the chain lines, as well as the size and spacing of the laid lines, differed for each mold, as did the design and placement of the watermarks. Since most codices written in the Middle Ages and Renaissance have no title pages, the text and the physical composition of the codex are used to determine its approximate date and its geographical origin. The slight variations in hand-produced paper can often be useful in this regard.

Watermarks

10 Beinecke MS 276
Julius Africanus, *Cestoi*
(in Greek)
Italy? ca. 1582

The distinctive watermarks in Beinecke MS 276 have helped in dating the volume. Although the colophon states that the text was transcribed by Andreas Darmarius, it does not mention the date of production. Comparison of these watermarks with watermarks from another manuscript, also signed by Darmarius and dated 5 April 1582, suggests that this prolific Renaissance scribe had at his disposal the same paper supply for both the Beinecke volume and the codex now preserved in Munich. It seems probable that the two manuscripts are nearly contemporaneous.

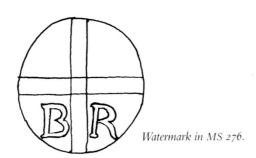

Watermark in MS 276.

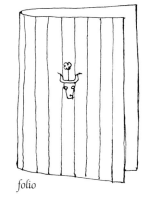

full sheet   folio   quarto   octavo

Folding a sheet of paper.

PRICKING AND RULING *The arrangement of the text and ornamentation in a medieval manuscript was carefully planned and executed. The first step was to determine the overall size of the book. Whether paper or parchment served as the support, the material had to be folded and cut to form the leaves of the codex. A single sheet of paper folded once forms a folio volume; folded twice the sheet yields a quarto, and three times an octavo volume. The position of the watermark was affected by each fold of the paper; the smaller the size of the volume, the more difficult to reconstruct the watermark from its visible portions.*

The cut sheets were usually arranged in groups of four or five and folded once to compose a quire or gathering. As a result each quire might have either eight or ten leaves, forming sixteen or twenty pages. A series of gatherings sewn together through the folds in the sheets made up the codex.

Once the leaves were cut and arranged into gatherings, each folio had to be planned with respect to its layout in columns and lines. In most codices, the pages were clearly ruled; but as a guide for the ruling, small holes were first made with a sharp instrument in the paper or parchment. These ruling holes, or prickings, were arranged in widely varying patterns according to time period, geographical region, and the practices of a specific monastery or workshop. Today prickings are not always visible in a manuscript, for they were normally located along the outer edges of the pages and were trimmed off in binding.

This fragmentary text of Aldhelm's *De laude virginitatis* was copied at the beginning of the ninth century—perhaps in Canterbury or Worcester to judge from the script. There are two rows of prickings for the horizontal rulings, one along the innermost vertical bounding line, which constitutes the left-hand margin of the text space, and one along the outermost. The presence of two vertical columns of prickings on each text page is a feature of early manuscripts produced in England and Ireland and usually indicates that the leaves were ruled after they were folded to form a quire. Some of the prickings seem to have been made with a sharp pointed tool that punctured the parchment, but others are horizontal slits made with a small knife. A peculiar feature of MS 401 is the presence of two horizontal rulings for each line of text; the scribe has written the body of the letterforms between them, with only ascenders and descenders crossing the guidelines.

In the richly illustrated copy of the *Speculum humanae salvationis* from fifteenth-century England the prickings are prominent in the upper, outer, and lower margins,

Double and Single Pricking

11 Beinecke MS 401
Aldhelm, *De laude virginitatis* (fragments)
England, early 9th century

12 Beinecke MS 27
Speculum humanae salvationis; pseudo-Bonaventura, *Meditationes de passione Christi*
England, early 15th century

*Scheme of prickings
and rulings in MS 401.*

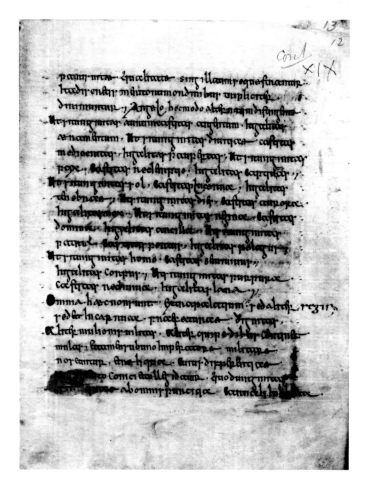

11 *MS 401, f. 12r.*

revealing that the double sheets of parchment were ruled before they were folded. A single extra pricking in the outer margin defines the lower edge of the space for the drawings.

Ruling with a Stylus

13 Beinecke MS 402
Gospels of Matthew
and Mark
Freising, first half of the 11th century

In the earliest parchment manuscripts, a sharp stylus was used to rule the leaves. Lines executed in this manner have a fine furrow on one side of the leaf and a raised ridge on the other. It was possible to rule more than one page at a time if enough pressure were applied to the stylus. Rulings drawn with a stylus on the hair side of the parchment delineate the page format of Beinecke MS 402, an eleventh-century codex of the Gospels of Matthew and Mark. Produced at Freising in southern Germany, probably around the middle of the eleventh century, the manuscript was copied in twenty-four long lines of text; single horizontal lines mark the upper and lower boundaries of the written space, while double vertical bounding lines appear on each side of the text. Single vertical rulings in both the inner and outer margins designate the area for the Ammonian sections that identify parallels between corresponding verses in the Gospels.

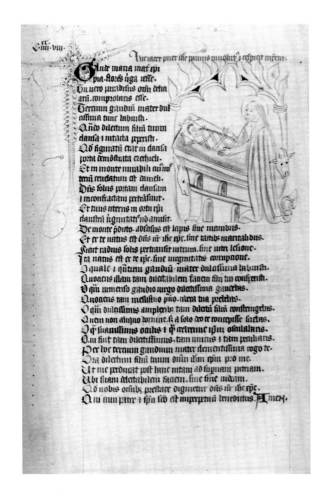

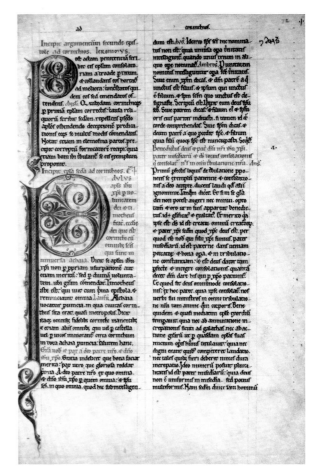

12 *Prickings in MS 27, f. 88v.*

14 *Crayon rulings in MS 154, f. 72r.*

Sometime during the twelfth century the stylus was replaced as the instrument for ruling parchment in most areas of Europe—except in Italy where it prevailed into the Renaissance. Rulings were now drawn either with an implement made three-quarters of lead and one-quarter of bronze that produced a grey line similar to that made by a pencil, or with a "crayon" that left a brown, speckled line. With either procedure, each leaf had to be ruled on both sides since the lines did not show through. In the fifteenth century, rulings in various shades of ink, including red or violet, formed appealing decorative frames for the text. This twelfth-century manuscript of Robert of Bridlington's Bible commentaries was boldly ruled in crayon before the text was written in two columns. An additional line in the upper margin provided space for the running titles. The distinctive placement of prickings and rulings, as well as the style of the elegant Romanesque initials, will help to attribute the codex to a specific center of manuscript production in northern England.

Crayon Rulings

14 Beinecke MS 154

Robert of Bridlington, *Catenae* on Romans, 1 Corinthians, and 2 Corinthians (incomplete)

Northern England, second half of the 12th century

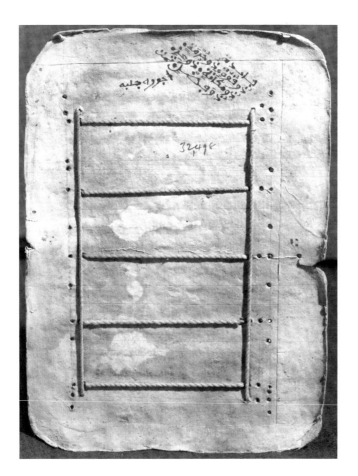

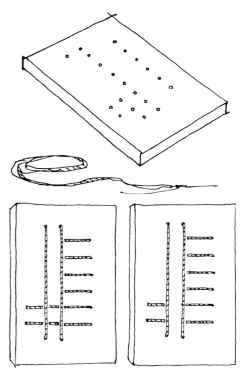

*Ruling board, unstrung and strung,
with two possible arrangements.*

1 5 *Ruling board. Arabic MS 198.*

Ruling Board

1 5   Beinecke Arabic MS 198
Khalil ibn Ishak, *al Jundi*
al-Mukhtasar, Manual of
Maliki law

18th century

Another technique for ruling leaves involved a mechanical device called a ruling board. In Arabic manuscripts of the Middle Ages and later, sheets of paper or parchment were set on top of a frame (Arabic: *mastara*) composed of parallel strings. The page was then firmly rubbed with the thumb or with a burnishing instrument so that the strings left a clear impression. Beinecke Arabic MS 198 has a *mastara* attached to the cover of the binding. There are multiple sets of holes in the cover, through which the movable strings can be threaded to change both the proportions and size of the written space and the distance between the lines of text. The paper leaves of the manuscript display several physical formats that correspond to the various string settings of the frame. Recent discoveries in codicology have revealed that a similar principle was used for ruling parchment manuscripts in Italy during the Renaissance. When a manuscript has been ruled on a board, there is usually a break in the horizontal lines at the point where they would normally intersect vertical rulings, since the strings for the horizontal rulings run under the vertical strings.

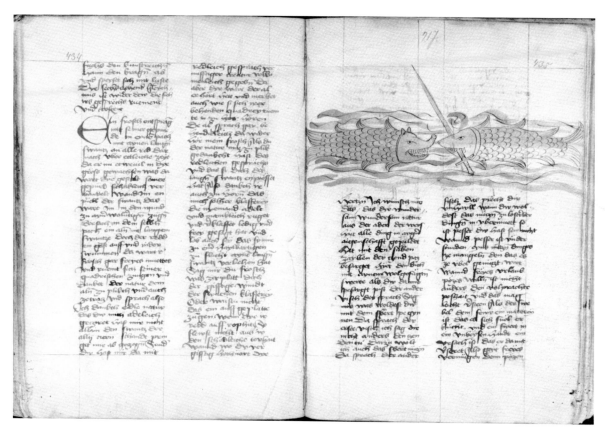

17 *Drawings extending beyond rulings. MS 653, ff. 216v–217r.*

Two simpler methods of defining the written space were used in the late Middle Ages and Renaissance for manuscripts of modest appearance. In Italy in the second half of the fifteenth century leaves were often folded in quarters lengthwise to define left and right margins, a technique used for Marston MS 77. It was certainly easier and quicker to fold the sheets than to rule all the lines, but the result was less satisfactory. The pages remained disfigured by the accordion-like pleats, and the scribe, unless cautious, could easily wander off track. The number of lines per page and the spacing of the script vary considerably in this manuscript because of the lack of horizontal text rulings.

The other ruling technique was to draw only the outer limits of the text columns. Beinecke MS 653 contains, among other works, a German translation of the *Speculum sapientiae*, a treatise on virtues and vices in the form of dialogues, usually between animals, but also between trees, natural elements, and people. There was little coordination between the individuals who ruled the pages and those who wrote and decorated them. Each leaf was ruled in precisely the same manner, with single horizontal and vertical lines defining the two columns. Throughout the treatise the artist had to draw the illustrations in the limited space allotted by the scribe and over the rulings for the columns. In this example two charming fish swim through the margins and across the guidelines.

Other Methods of Delimiting Space

16 Beinecke Marston MS 77
Pietro della Vigna, Letters
(*de gestis Friderici Romanorum imperatoris*)
and official documents
Italy, second half of the 15th century

17 Beinecke MS 653
Moralia: anonymous German religious work; pseudo-Avicenna, *De sectione venarum* (German tr.); *Speculum sapientiae* (German tr.); "Dye ansprach des tewffels gegen unsern herrn": anonymous religious poem
Germany, mid-15th century

Complex Ruling Patterns

18 Beinecke Marston MS 152

Pauline Epistles,
with commentary of
Gilbert de la Porrée
England, mid-12th century

Certain texts necessitated a more elaborate and sometimes asymmetrical presentation. Marston MS 152 contains the fourteen Pauline Epistles, accompanied by the commentary of Gilbert de la Porrée (d. 1154). Produced in England in the mid-twelfth century, the manuscript displays a *mise-en-page* that attempts to accommodate both the main text and the commentary. Each Epistle is boldly written in a narrow column about 58 mm. wide; for every line of the Bible there are two or more compact lines of commentary copied in a broad outer column which measures about 85 mm. in width. The rulings for the commentary were drawn with a stylus, while those for the main text were added very faintly in lead or crayon. Since the ruling format for each leaf is tailored to its specific contents, the relationship between epistle and commentary had to be carefully articulated before either the script or the intricate decorated initials were executed.

18 *Marston MS 152, f. 86v.*

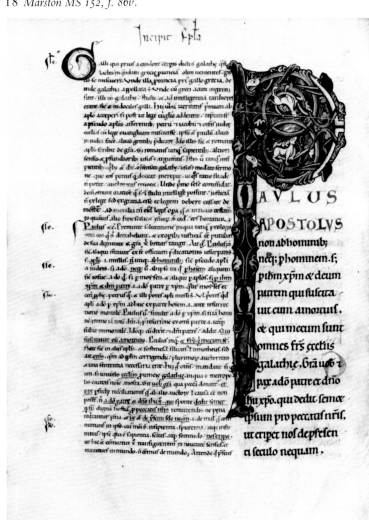

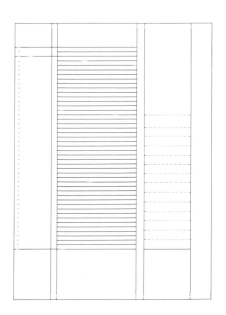

*Ruling patterns
in Marston MS 152,
f. 86v.*

SCRIBES *After the leaves had been pricked and ruled, it was the scribe's task to copy the text as accurately as possible, and to leave the appropriate amount of space for headings, initials, or illustrations. Copying a complete codex by hand was physically demanding and could require months of intensive labor by one or more scribes. Manuscripts occasionally allude to the copyist's plight. Nicolaus of Rhodes records his grim lament in the colophon of Beinecke MS 300, completed in June 1642:*

> *The hand which wrote this book will decay, alas!, and will become dust. It will come to the tomb which is the bane of all flesh. But we are all a part of Christ. Pray to the Lord that forgiveness of sins flows freely. Yea, I shall enter where, after lamentation, have gone our brothers and fathers. Receive my pitiable prayer, o heavenly Host . . . woe is me.*

We can speculate that the skills and perseverance of the scribe were not always appreciated, and that his life was not always a happy one. In at least one monastery of the Middle Ages penances were imposed on scribes who were negligent in the performance of their duties: 130 genuflections to the monk who disregarded the correct spelling, accentuation, and punctuation of the manuscript he was copying, but only thirty for one who broke his pen in a fit of anger! If a copyist disobeyed the instructions of the head scribe, he was banished from church for two days, a severe punishment for a monk.

19 *Luke the Evangelist as scribe. MS 150, vol. 2, f. 3v.*

Author as Scribe

19 Beinecke MS 150
"Seymour" Gospels
(in Greek)
*Byzantium, first half of the
11th century*

Many manuscripts of the Middle Ages contain miniatures depicting the scribe, or frequently the author, seated at a stand or desk, a roll or codex placed in front of him, with pen in one hand and ink or knife in the other. A series of illuminations in Beinecke MS 150, a two-volume manuscript of the Greek Gospels from the eleventh century, shows three of the Evangelists at work (the miniature of Matthew is missing). They sit at desks that contain various materials and implements for writing: scrolls, ink pots, knives, quills, and a flat tray-like container with both red and black ink. Mark balances on his knee an unopened codex with a jewel-encrusted binding while raising his right hand to his chin as if contemplating the task before him. John, seated on an elaborate wickerwork chair, has a writing desk with a stand attached to its top. He unfurls one roll on which is written, in red, the opening words of his Gospel, while another scroll, devoid of script, lies partially unrolled on top of the stand. Luke is shown in the act of writing his Gospel into a book held on his lap.

20 Beinecke MS 214
Petrus Comestor,
Historia scholastica
France, 1229

At the beginning of Petrus Comestor's *Historia scholastica* are two exceptionally fine illuminations, the lower one showing the author as a scribe seated in front of two writing stands, the one on the right presumably holding either his notes or a rough draft of his work, from which he is making a fair copy. In 1229 another man named Peter gave this codex to the Benedictine monastery of Mont Saint-Quentin. A full-page inscription and book curse records the donation:

> In the name of the Father and the Son and the Holy Spirit, Amen. In the one thousand two hundred twenty-ninth year from the incarnation of our Lord, Peter, of all monks the least significant, gave this book to the most blessed martyr, Saint Quentin. If anyone should steal it, let him know that on the Day of Judgment the most sainted martyr himself will be the accuser against him before the face of our Lord Jesus Christ.

Since most people in the Middle Ages were illiterate, the scribe occupied an important place within the monastery and in society. Certain scribes, who served both as notaries for legal and business documents and as copyists for manuscript books, might know more than one style of writing for each required task. The Beinecke Library has two unusual items that give some insight into the nature of teaching calligraphy and the range of scribal expertise.

Writing Exercise

21 P.CtYBR inv. 1253
Front: accounts;
back: writing exercise
Egypt, 2nd or 3rd century

This papyrus fragment from the second or third century records a schoolboy's writing exercise. The young man was assigned the task of copying four sentences from Demosthenes, the Palatine Anthology, Homer, and Xenophon. The awkwardly formed letters suggest that he had not yet mastered the finer points of writing the Greek alphabet. The second sentence of the exercise includes the twenty-four letters of the Greek alphabet:

αβροχιτων δε φυλαξ θηρωζυγωκαμψιμετωπος
(The soft-garmented, beast-yoking, forehead-bending guard)

Like most abecedarian formulas, this one makes little sense, but the words helped to teach writing, or assisted an experienced scribe in limbering up before starting the day's transcriptions.

20 *Petrus Comestor as scribe. MS 214, f. 3v.*

21 *Schoolboy's writing exercise*
on the back of a papyrus document from Egypt.

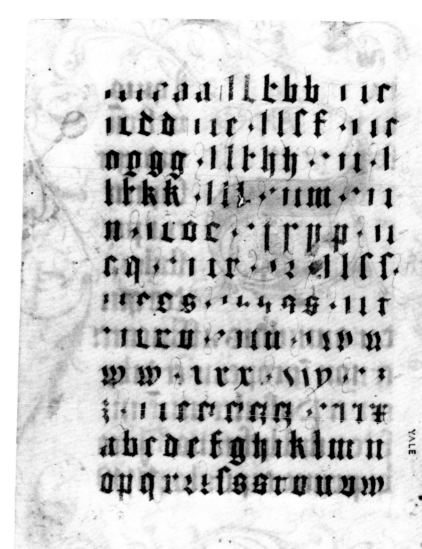

22 *Letterforms written
stroke by stroke.
MS 439, ff. 1v–2r.*

Pattern Book

22 Beinecke MS 439
Gregorius Bock,
Scribal pattern book

Swabia, ca. 1510–17

In the later Middle Ages, when there was a proliferation of scripts for Latin, a scribe might prepare a specimen book to illustrate for potential customers the various styles of writing he knew. The scribal pattern book of Gregorius Bock contains the alphabet in various scripts and examples of decorative initials ranging from the austere capitals of Roman monuments to large fanciful capitals that incorporate human and animal grotesques. Toward the beginning of this volume, Bock shows stroke by stroke how to write each letter of formal Gothic bookhand. In the case of the letter *o*, where his sequence of strokes is wrong, he corrects his error by numbering them in their proper order.

SCRIPTS *Medieval scripts were written according to established rules and models. Letter-forms, abbreviations, ligatures, and punctuation varied, depending upon time and place. Function also affected script. More formal styles were common for the Bible, liturgical manuscripts, and deluxe volumes, while books composed in vernacular languages or designed for personal use were frequently executed in less carefully articulated scripts.*

The capital letterforms, or majuscules, still in use today can be traced to the Romans and the inscriptions on their monuments. Characterized by precision and elegance of line, these letters were first painted on the stone surface with broad brushes; stonecutters, using chisels, followed the guidelines. The scribes of the Middle Ages, putting pen to parchment or paper, adapted

23 *Roman square capitals on simulated marble stele. MS 391, ff. 6v–7r.*

these majuscule forms for early manuscripts, distinguishing more carefully between the thick lines of the vertical and oblique (or curving) strokes and the thin lines of the horizontal strokes than was possible on stone. Roman square capitals of this design were not wholly suitable for a text hand, for they took much time to write and required a lot of space, but they were popular for headings in later manuscripts and were often so used in the Renaissance.

Roman Square Capitals

23 Beinecke MS 391
Ludovico Lazarelli, *Fasti christianae religionis*
Italy, late 15th century

An elegantly illuminated codex produced in Italy at the end of the fifteenth century illustrates one technique for incorporating Roman square capitals into the design of the page. After a dedication letter to the patron of the work and a brief "dialogue" between the author and his Muse, the text opens with an inscription in gold square capitals on a marble-patterned panel, providing the author's name, Ludovico Lazarelli, the patron's name, Ferdinand of Aragon, King of Naples (d. 1494), and the title of the work, *Fasti christianae religionis*. The unidentified artist, influenced by the Renaissance fascination with archeology and antique sculpture, attempted to replicate early Roman monumental inscriptions. The square capitals are expertly rendered in the three-dimensional space of the marble stele.

Of greater importance for understanding the development of Latin writing is a second style of majuscule called rustic capitals. The letters are narrower and can be written more quickly, with gentle curves often replacing the rigid angles of square capitals. Rustic capitals were employed with square capitals as display scripts, for example in MS 413 *(catalogue number 28), a handsome manuscript of the ninth century.*

Roman cursive, or running hand, concentrated more on speed than clarity: in the interest of writing quickly, the scribe often ran letters together. Cursive hands were used by the Romans for wall graffiti, rough drafts, and other texts, such as this legal document. Probably from the first half of the seventh century, the papyrus fragment records a donation of property by a woman named Wiliwa, who dictated the text to a public scribe. As in most early texts, the words and sentences are not separated by spaces or punctuation, making the document hard for us to decipher. With the words separated, three complete lines read:

> susteneas cunctis femineis sex priuelegiis et ignorantiae
> legum frustrationibus ex omni documentum; a quam au-
> tem donationem d(o)l(o) m(alo) uim et metu et circumscribtionem

Roman Cursive

24   P.CtYBR inv. 2125
Fragment of a deed of donation
Ravenna, 613–41

Roman uncial script developed from rustic capitals but was influenced by Greek writing and incorporated certain everyday letterforms. Uncial was employed between about 350 and 800, as Roman square and rustic capitals gradually fell into disuse. Aesthetically pleasing and easy to read, uncial was quicker to write than capitals. The use of uncial script was fostered by the Christian Church for the production of Bibles and the texts of the Church Fathers; as a result, Christian books of this period have an appearance distinctly different from classical texts. This fragment of the Gospel according to St. Luke, written in a large but gracefully executed uncial script, is from a Bible produced in Italy in the fourth quarter of the seventh century. The parchment is pale, providing good contrast for the precisely drawn letterforms. While this uncial has the monumental quality of capitals, it is somewhat rounder and less symmetrical in appearance. The letter *m*, for instance, consists of three gently curving strokes, instead of four angular strokes as in square or rustic capitals. Though many of the uncial letters are formed like majuscules, not all are of similar size and proportions, for ascending and descending strokes often extend above and below the line of writing.

Latin Uncial

25   Beinecke MS 481, Box 1, no. 1
Gospel of Luke: 12.54–56, 59–13.2, 4–6, 8–11 (fragment)
Italy, fourth quarter of the 7th century

At approximately the same time that uncial script emerged from rustic capitals, provincial chanceries of the late Roman Empire were using local, or so-called national, varieties of cursive script similar to that found in the papyrus fragment from Ravenna. In most instances the local scripts were easier to write than uncial or capitals, yet they were more calligraphic than the Roman cursive of late antiquity.

The first of two examples of local script is from the abbey of Luxeuil near Belfort in the ancient kingdom of Burgundy. Founded by the Irish Saint Columbanus around 590, Luxeuil emerged as one of the great centers of Merovingian culture during the

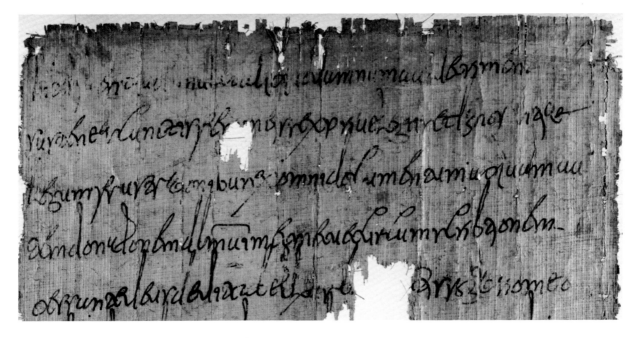

24 *Roman cursive in a papyrus document from Ravenna.*

25 *Latin uncial. MS 481, Box 2, no. 1.*

Luxeuil Minuscule

26 Beinecke MS 481, Box 1, no. 2

St. Augustine, *Sermo* 190.3 (fragment)

Luxeuil, second half of 7th century

seventh and eighth centuries. It was the mother house of many abbeys throughout France and was itself an important writing center. The minuscule script developed and written at Luxeuil bears a marked resemblance to the Roman cursive from which it is ultimately derived, but the strokes of each letterform are controlled and restrained. Luxeuil script is the first known calligraphic minuscule used for writing Latin codices. Among the many fragments catalogued as Beinecke MS 481 is a single leaf from a codex written at Luxeuil in the second half of the seventh century. Although the leaf has suffered considerable damage, the text, a sermon by St. Augustine, remains legible.

26 *Luxeuil minuscule. MS 481, Box 1, no. 2.*

27 *Visigothic. MS 481, Box 1, no. 3.*

A second example of a local script occurs on a leaf copied in northeastern Spain toward the end of the ninth century. Between the eighth and eleventh centuries most Latin manuscripts produced in the Iberian peninsula were written in a script called Visigothic, with pronounced differences according to geographical regions. The styles of Visigothic prevalent in northern Spain revealed French influence as early as the ninth century, while the scripts originating in southern Spain remained closer to their roots in Roman cursive well into the eleventh century. The letters in the Beinecke fragment are handsomely formed and carefully executed; though some letters are joined in combinations called ligatures, many, such as *o* and *m*, stand alone. Because

Visigothic

27 Beinecke MS 481, Box 1, no. 3

St. Basil the Great, *Regula*, Latin tr. Rufinus (fragment)

Northeastern Spain, late 9th century

words are sometimes divided and punctuation is used, the overall effect of the page is more spacious than in Luxeuil minuscule, and the link to Roman cursive less pronounced.

After the collapse of the Roman Empire in 476, the most significant event to affect manuscript production occurred in the reign of Charlemagne. Born around 725, Charlemagne ruled between 771 and 814, first as King of the Franks and later as Emperor of the West, actively promoting the spread of Christianity and the advancement of education. Under the auspices of Charlemagne and Alcuin, an English Benedictine monk and the abbot of Tours, a new script, which we now call Carolingian minuscule, was fostered and eventually spread throughout Europe, coexisting with or superseding local and national styles of writing.

Carolingian Minuscule

28 Beinecke MS 413
Capitularies of
Charlemagne, Louis the
Pious, and Charles the Bald
Northeastern France, ca. 873

Although the precise origins of Carolingian minuscule as well as the reasons for its development are subject to debate, its characteristics are easy to define. Beinecke MS 413, produced in northeastern France shortly after 873, contains the capitularies of Charlemagne, of his son Louis the Pious, and of Charles the Bald. The script, an example of fully developed Carolingian minuscule, is uncluttered and neat, and most of the cursive elements in the letterforms, including ligatures, have been eliminated. The ascenders and descenders of letters do not extend far beyond the line of writing; and, equally important, both word separation and punctuation have become standard practices. The new minuscule soon gained acceptance in Charlemagne's empire, although some of the old styles of writing were retained in headings. On the leaf reproduced here the scribe has used rustic capitals in the first two lines and larger square capitals for the next three. The lines of majuscules form a bridge between the bold decorative initial and the body of the text in Carolingian minuscule. This concept of arranging scripts hierarchically is a feature of manuscript production from the Carolingian period through the Renaissance.

Late Carolingian Minuscule

29 Beinecke Marston MS 157
St. Augustine, *Confessiones*
England, early 12th century

The Carolingian Empire disintegrated by the tenth century; yet Carolingian minuscule, in one form or another, lasted into the middle of the twelfth century, developing into a more calligraphic style characterized by finishing strokes, or serifs, on the various letterforms. The result was a script more uniform and formal in appearance than the minuscule of the ninth century. A comparison of this copy of St. Augustine's *Confessions* produced in England toward the beginning of the twelfth century with the manuscript of capitularies makes the evolution of the script apparent. In the later manuscript, most ascenders and descenders have fine oblique lines at their tops and bottoms, and letters sit along the rulings. The writing on the page is more compressed, yet most words are carefully separated by spaces or punctuation.

During the twelfth century, Carolingian minuscule was slowly replaced by the Gothic script that developed from it. The term "Gothic" encompasses many varieties of Latin writing ranging from the bold formal hands of some deluxe manuscripts to the highly abbreviated cursive hands used in chanceries and school texts. The transformation was gradual: what one scholar labels late Carolingian, another may call early Gothic. There is no doubt, though, that fully

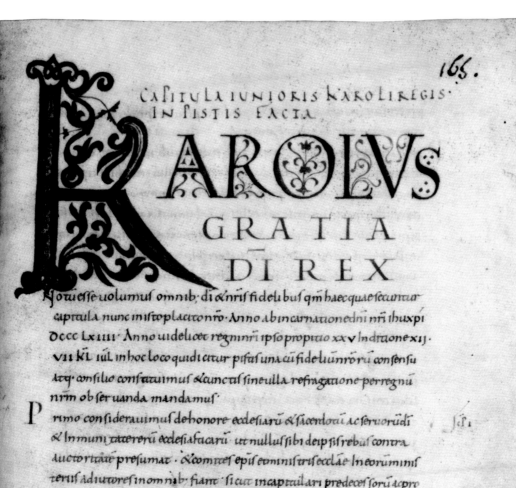

165.

CAPITULA IUNIORIS KAROLI REGIS·
IN PISTIS FACTA

KAROLVS
GRATIA
DĪ REX

Notu esse uolumus omnib; di & nris fidelibus qm haec quae secuntur
captula nunc in isto placito nro· Anno ab incarnatione dni nri ihuxpi
Dccc Lxiiii· Anno uidelicet regni nri ipso propitio xxv Indiaone xij·
vii Kl iul· in hoc loco qui dicitur pisas una cu fideliu nro ru consensu
atq; consilio constituimus & cunctis sineulla refragatione perregnu
nrm obseruanda mandamus·

P rimo considerauimus de honore ecclesiaru & sacerdotu ac seruoru di
& In munitateroru ecclesiafacaru· ut nullus sibi de ipsis rebus contra
auctoritate presumat· & comites epis comini tris ecclae In eorum minis
teriis adiutores in omniab; fiant· sicut in captulari predecessoru ac pro
genitoru nroru continetur In secundo libro cap xxiii· Et quia ciq co
mitu uel ministroru rei publice haec quae mandamus obseruare negle
xerit· si prima & secunda uice de his admonitus non se correxerit· uo
lumus ut neglegentia comitis ad nram notitia per epos et per missos
nros deferatur· & aliorum neglegentia per comites ad nram notitiam

28 *Text in Carolingian minuscule,
heading in rustic and square capitals.
MS 413, f. 83r.*

29 *Late Carolingian minuscule. Marston MS 157, f. 19v.*

developed *Gothic script prevailed in the thirteenth through fifteenth centuries and even served as the model for type design in some early printed books. The change has to do with the increasing demand, beginning around 1150, for manuscript books, especially in university towns like Paris, Bologna, and Oxford. It was necessary for scribes to conserve parchment and to write faster. While book production in the preceding centuries had taken place mainly in monastic communities, a new breed of secular professional scribe began to appear in university centers around 1200.*

Gothic Bookhands

30 Beinecke MS 81
Latin Bible (incomplete)
*England, second half of the
13th century*

Although Gothic scripts defy any simple system of taxonomy, the examples offered here illustrate three styles of Gothic bookhand. In the Latin Bible, the scribe has managed to compress fifty-two lines of text into each column, but the pages have a pleasing sense of regularity and balance. The writing is minute and compact, and certain strokes are joined, fusing one letterform to the next. This fusion or "biting" of letters is a hallmark of formal Gothic. The Gothic text scripts of Flanders, Germany, England, and northern France all emphasized a sharp and angular style in which the letters appeared to be woven together to form a line, hence the name given to the script, *littera textura* (Latin: *texere*, to weave). In the fourteenth and fifteenth centuries certain features of Gothic bookhand were exaggerated: letters become more ornate and denser in appearance, to save space words were more radically abbreviated than in earlier book scripts.

While northern scribes were practising angular styles of Gothic bookhand, the scribes of southern France and Italy stressed the uncluttered quality of Carolingian minuscule. The curving bows of Carolingian letters were not abandoned, nor were letters tightly fused. An excellent example of round Gothic, called *littera rotunda*

30 *Compact Gothic bookhand. MS 81, f. 214r.*

31 *Round Gothic bookhand from Italy. Marston MS 155, f. 70v.*

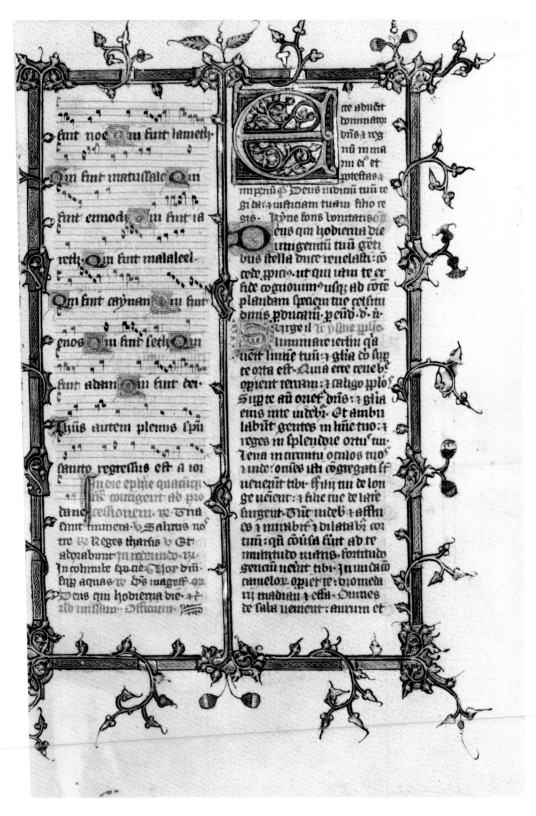

32 *Calligraphic Gothic bookhand from England. MS 286, f. 42r.*

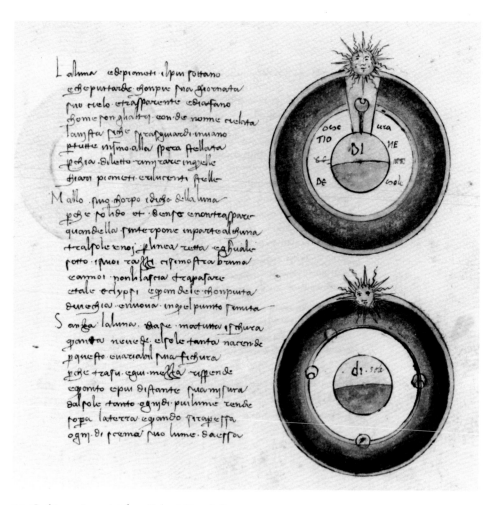

33 *Gothic cursive script from Italy. MS 328, f. 5r.*

because of its shape, is found in Beinecke Marston MS 155, a beautifully written and decorated manuscript produced in Bologna around 1325. The main text, Pope Boniface VIII's *Liber sextus decretalium*, was arranged in the middle of each leaf and surrounded by the extensive commentary of Johannes Andreae, written in a smaller script. At least one later hand added notes in the margins. The manuscript probably helped meet the growing demand for canon law texts at the University of Bologna during the fourteenth century. Even though the scribe has managed to crowd an extraordinary amount of text onto a single page, there is less tendency to link letters than in northern Gothic. The script retains the roundness and simplicity of Carolingian letterforms, while exhibiting the compression of Gothic.

At the same time that scribes were forsaking the more leisurely spaced Carolingian minuscule in favor of the compact Gothic bookhands, another trend stressed the calligraphic potential of Gothic script and its visual impact. Perhaps the most stylized Gothic writing is found in liturgical manuscripts from northern Europe. Beinecke MS 286 is a good illustration of a formal Gothic script used in England toward the end of the fourteenth century. This finely embellished Missal was copied in an elegant bookhand in which the words are carefully spaced across the lines. Each letter is precisely articulated, and the vertical strokes consistently end with pronounced serifs resembling little "feet." The sumptuous borders and initials, complementing the harmoniously executed script, show that the manuscript was an expensive production.

Gothic Cursive

33 Beinecke MS 328
Gregorio (or Leonardo?)
Dati, *La Sfera*
Florence, third quarter of the 15th century

The term "Gothic" is also applied to more functional styles of writing—scripts that could be written more rapidly than formal bookhands to produce less costly volumes. Toward the close of the twelfth century, a neat cursive developed; initially used for legal documents and business records, this Gothic hand was also employed to transcribe books, particularly those composed in vernacular languages. The Beinecke copy of Dati's treatise on astronomy and navigation, produced in Florence in the third quarter of the fifteenth century, was transcribed on paper and decorated with tinted diagrams, drawings, and maps, all of average quality. Some letters are joined while others are written separately. This stylized Gothic script was well suited to the functional nature of the manuscript.

Fifteenth-century Italy was the home of a revolution in the history of writing comparable to that which occurred under Charlemagne. The new script, termed "humanistic," was favored by the scholars of the Italian Renaissance. It revived the clean lines of the Carolingian minuscule practiced in Italy during the twelfth century, avoiding the features that made Gothic hands difficult to read. In the decades immediately after its evolution shortly before 1400, humanistic script became the chief style of writing in Florence for Latin texts and rapidly spread throughout the rest of Italy.

Humanistic Bookhand

34 Beinecke Marston MS 52
Suetonius, *De vita Caesarum*
Bologna, mid-15th century

35 Beinecke MS 382
Psalter (bifolium): Psalms 113.2–117.1 (fragment)
Central Italy, mid-12th century

Marston MS 52 illustrates why humanistic bookhand became so popular after more than two centuries of Gothic. This handsomely decorated text, written in Bologna in the middle of the fifteenth century by the scribe Simon Carpaneti, is easy to read. Letters are simply written and neatly spaced, there are few ligatures, and the generous margins and page proportions are reminiscent of Carolingian codices. Even the design of the white vine-stem initial on multicolored ground was imitated from the earlier liturgical and patristic texts of Tuscany and central Italy, as is clearly shown by a comparison of Marston MS 52 with Beinecke MS 382, a bifolium of a Psalter produced in the middle of the twelfth century. The design of the foliage scrollwork is more intricate in the later manuscript, yet its derivation from a twelfth-century model is obvious.

Humanistic Cursive

36 Beinecke Marston MS 39
Cicero, *De oratore*, *Pro Milone*, and *Pro Q. Ligario*
Italy, 1453

A second sort of humanistic script, which coexisted with the formal bookhand, was introduced in the second quarter of the fifteenth century by the noted humanist Niccolò Niccoli. Both quicker and more legible than Gothic, the new cursive was adopted by notaries because it derived ultimately from the Gothic chancery scripts they normally used. By the mid-fifteenth century, humanistic cursive was respectable enough for even deluxe manuscripts. The scribe Phylippus Corbizus, who signed and dated Marston MS 39, wrote a fine upright humanistic cursive. Although most letters have been linked so that the scribe need not lift his pen between strokes, the hand is still crisp and legible.

Ermanicus C cesaris pr drusi &
minoris antonie filius a tiberio
patruo adoptatus questuram qn
quenio anteq̃ per leges liceret &
post eam consulatu statim gessit.
Missusq̃, ad exercitu in germani
am. excessu augusti nuntiato le
giones uniuersas impatorem tiberium ptinacissime recusa
tes & sibi sumam rei·pu·deferentes incertum pietate ac con
stantia maiore compescuit atq̃, hoste mox deuicto triũpha
uit. Consul dẽn iterum creatus. ac priusq̃ honorem inirẽ
ad componendum orientis statum expulsus cum armenie
regem deuicisset. capadociamq̃, in prūincie formam rede

34 *Humanistic bookhand and vine-stem initial. Marston MS 52, f. 83v.*

et iustus·et deus nr miseretur·
Custodiens paruulos dñs·humiliat'
sũ·et liberauit me·
Conuertere anima mẽa inrequiẽ tuã·
quia dñs benefecit tibi·
Quia eripuit animã mẽa de morte·
oculos meos a lacrimis·pedes
meos a lapsu·
Placebo dño·inregione uiuoʒ·
cxv. ALLELVIA·
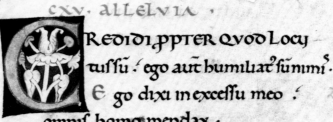
Redidi ppter qvod locy
tussũ·ego aut humiliat' sũnimi·
Ego dixi in excessu meo·
omnis homo mendax·

35 *Carolingian model for humanistic script and decoration. MS 382, f. 2r.*

ausam conferre in ipso: cum afferre plura si cuperes non queas.
Tum vero inquit catulus collegisti omnia quantum ego possum iudi
care ita diuinitus: ut non a grecis didicisse: sed eos ipsos hec docere
posse uideare. Me quidem istius sermonis participem esse factum
gaudeo: ac uellem: ut meus gener sodalis tuus hortensius adfu —
isset quem quidem ego confido omnibus istis laudibus quas tu
oratione complexus es excellentem fore. Et aussus fore ut dicis inquit.
ego uero esse tum iudico: et tum iudicaui: cum me consule in senatu
causam defendit africe: nuper os et magis cum pro bythinie rege
dixit. Quamobrem uides catule: nihil eos istis adolescentuli: neque
a natura: neque a doctrina deesse. eo os magis est tibi cotta: et tibi su —
lpicia uigilandum ac laborandum: tibi cum ille mediocris orator
uestre subcrescit etati: sed et ingenio praui: et studio flagranti.
et doctrina eximia: et memoria singulari. Cui quamquam faueo.
tu illum etati sue prestare cupio. Vobis uero illum tanto minorez
peruincere uix honestum est. Sed iam surgamus inquit: nos os
curemus: et aliquando ab hac contentione disputationis animos
nostros animos L A X E M V S.

36 *Humanistic cursive. Marston MS 39, f. 121v.*

DECORATION *By the time the codex was ready to be decorated, many decisions had already been made, either by the individual who planned the overall presentation or by the scribe who copied the text. It was necessary to allocate the proper amount of space for script and decoration, even in the simplest manuscript. Decoration ranged from small, plain initials and titles in red or other colors to delicately painted borders and historiated letters. The finest codices often contained full-page illuminations by well-known artists. The decoration clarified the physical presentation of the text and, in many manuscripts, illustrated the written word with visual images.*

Instructions for the Rubricator

37 Beinecke MS 315
I. Honorius of Autun, *Gemma animae*; II. pseudo-Hugh of St. Victor, *Speculum de mysteriis ecclesiae*; III. Jean Beleth, *Summa*

England, I. and II. fourth quarter of the 12th century; III. late 12th or early 13th century

Scribes usually left instructions for the workers who followed, especially for rubricators, who added the headings or portions of the text to be written in red—the rubrics—after the text proper was finished. Normally these notes would be erased or trimmed when the codex was bound, but in many manuscripts they are still visible. In MS 315, a copy of Jean Beleth's *Summa* written in England at the end of the twelfth century or beginning of the thirteenth, the scribe added notes to the rubricator in the inner margins, perhaps in the belief that they would be buried in the gutter of the binding. The scribe also left instructions for the person who painted the plain red and blue letters at the beginning of each chapter. In both the inner and outer margins a simple guide letter in black ink told the decorator which letter to place in the empty space.

The earliest decorative initials, only slightly larger than the script itself, apparently appeared at the top of each leaf, without regard to the text divisions. Eventually initials assumed a position somewhere between script and decoration. Any initial, plain or complex, might signal the beginning of a chapter, book, or verse. More elaborate codices incorporated a variety of initial types to divide the text hierarchically: the more lavish the initial, the more important the textual division. Nor did the initial letter always remain within the block of written space; often it was moved out into the margin to increase its impact. From the seventh to the twelfth century, an important period for decorated letters, the initial could serve as the primary artistic element.

Aniconic Initials

38 Beinecke MS 414
Latin Bible (second part of a two-volume Bible)

Aquitaine or Limousin, early 12th century

The elegant aniconic initials in this twelfth-century Latin Bible constitute the main ornamentation of the text. Each decorative initial is outlined in black ink and filled with intertwining foliage, interlace knots, and sometimes dragon heads. Set against irregular red, blue, green, and yellow panelled grounds, the initials display seemingly infinite permutations of twisting scrollwork designs. Foliate and zoomorphic elements such as those used in MS 414 were persistent motifs throughout the historical evolution of the decorated initial.

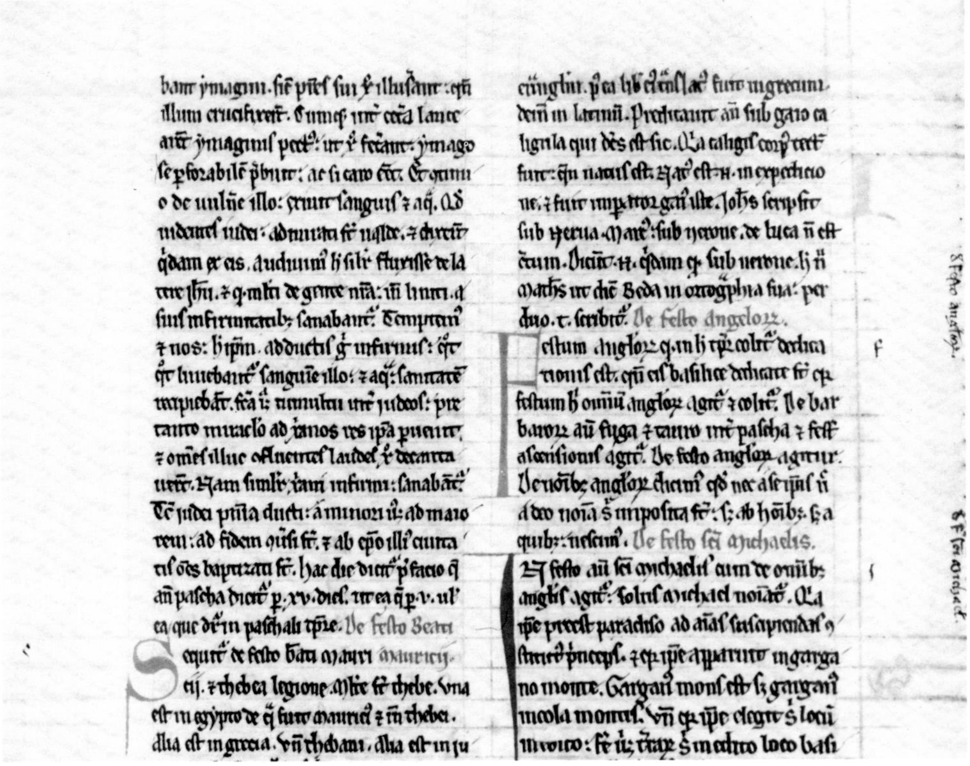

37 *Instructions to the rubricator, perpendicular to text, and guide letters for decorative initials. MS 315, f. 117v.*

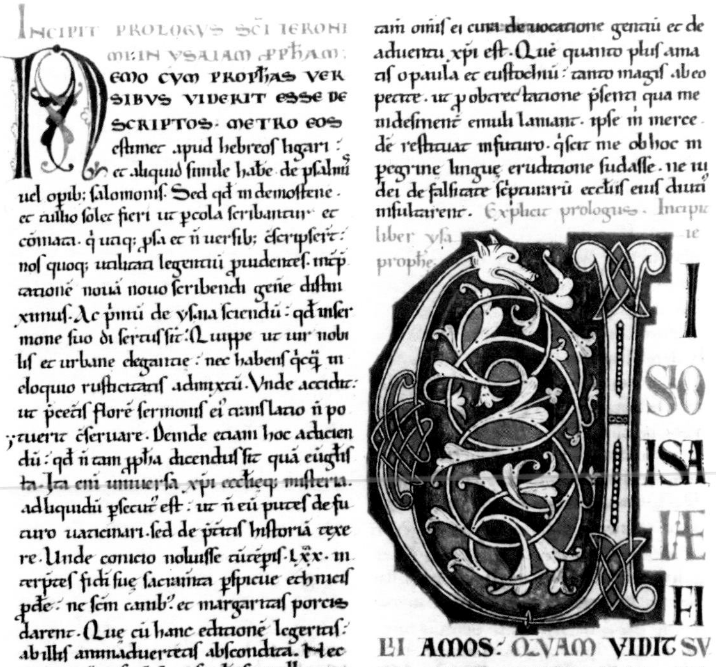

38 *Aniconic initial. MS 414, f. 1r.*

Pen-flourished initials, popular in the thirteenth through fifteenth centuries, might be only one or two lines high, but the flourishing designs—drawn with a quill rather than a brush—could extend the entire length of the page and into the margin. Three manuscripts from different regions illustrate the range of flourished designs for initials. Beinecke MS 111, an attractive copy of Jacobus de Voragine's *Legenda aurea* produced in northern Italy at the end of the fourteenth century or beginning of the fifteenth, has elaborate flourished initials, expertly drawn with intricate designs in red and blue, occasionally incorporating two shades of green. Yet initials such as these did not demand either exceptional creativity or imagination, since they were composed of patterns that could be repeated endlessly in all the codices executed in the same workshop. If the decorator followed a pattern book, he needed only patience and a steady hand.

On a slightly less accomplished level are the flourished initials in the Spanish Bible. The bodies of the letters contain tightly swirling curlicue and paisley-like patterns, punctuated by delicate dots in a contrasting color. The neatly articulated pen strokes that gently cascade down the margin appear frequently in Spanish flourished initials.

The third example of flourished initials, from a fourteenth-century Anglo-Norman manuscript produced in England, illustrates a hierarchy of decoration. In Pierre de Peckham's *La lumière as Lais* each verse of the poem has an initial highlighted with red or a single-line initial in blue. The more significant text divisions are marked by rubrics accompanied by a two-line initial, either blue with red pen-work designs or gold with blue designs. The beginning of the third book has a large initial showing the master explaining the poem to his student. Every detail of this page was planned well before the scribe began his task. The line-fillers, which justify the right-hand margins of the text, may also be helpful in ascribing the manuscript to a particular workshop. Some line-fillers, such as three in Beinecke MS 400, were signed by the proud artist: Petrus Gilberti.

Signed line-filler. MS 400, f. 102v.

During the twelfth century an artistic movement toward pictorial narrative influenced manuscript decoration throughout Europe. Figures became common both within the body of large initials and in miniatures. Instead of decorative letters composed almost exclusively of plant and vine motifs, artists painted historiated initials that contained a narrative or allegorical picture. The pictorial representation in the interior of the initial became the focal point of the decoration; the letter itself, separated from the text to which it belonged, functioned primarily as a frame for figurative art and secondarily as the first letter of text.

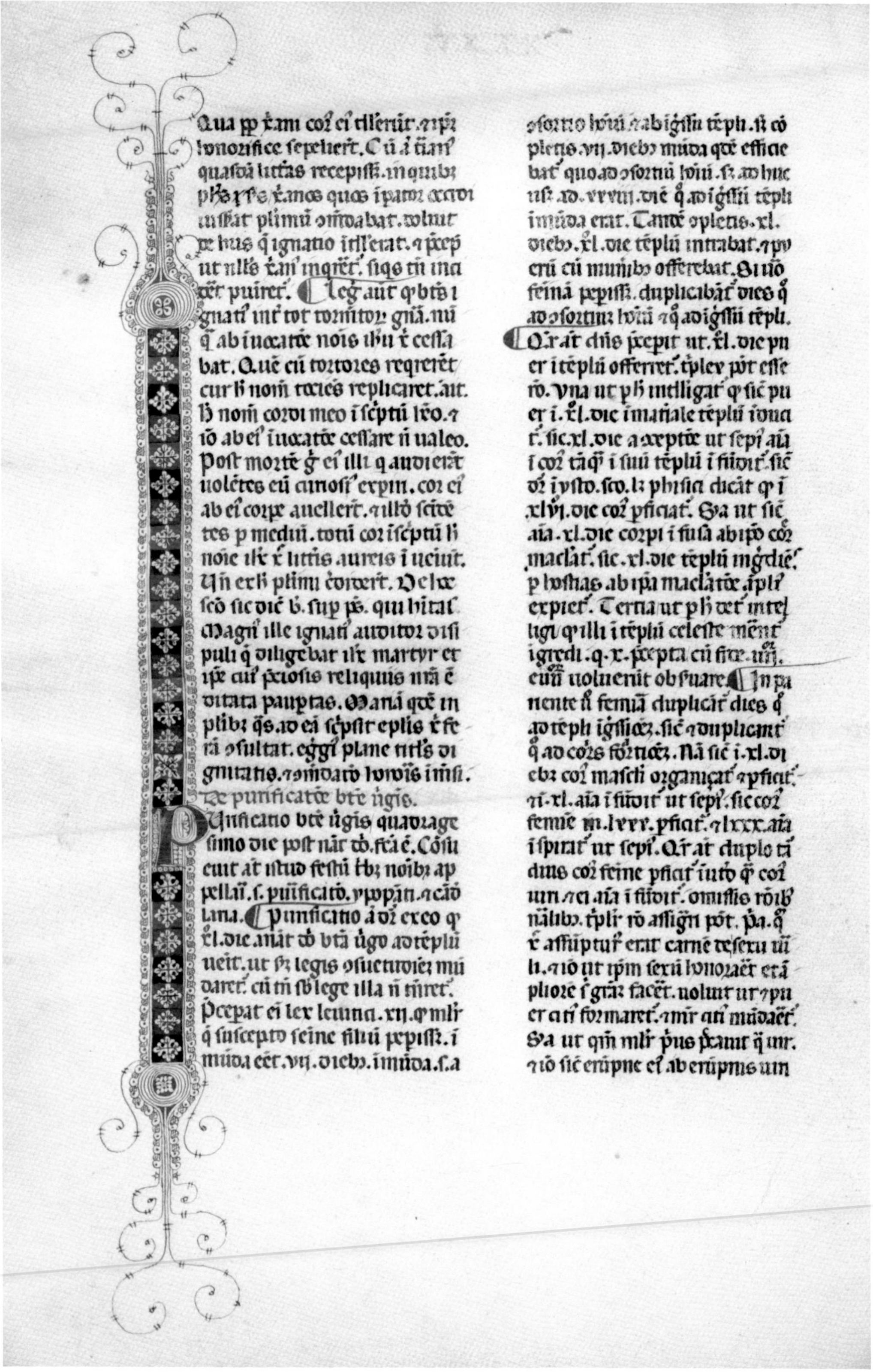

39 *Flourished initial. MS 111, f. 52v.*

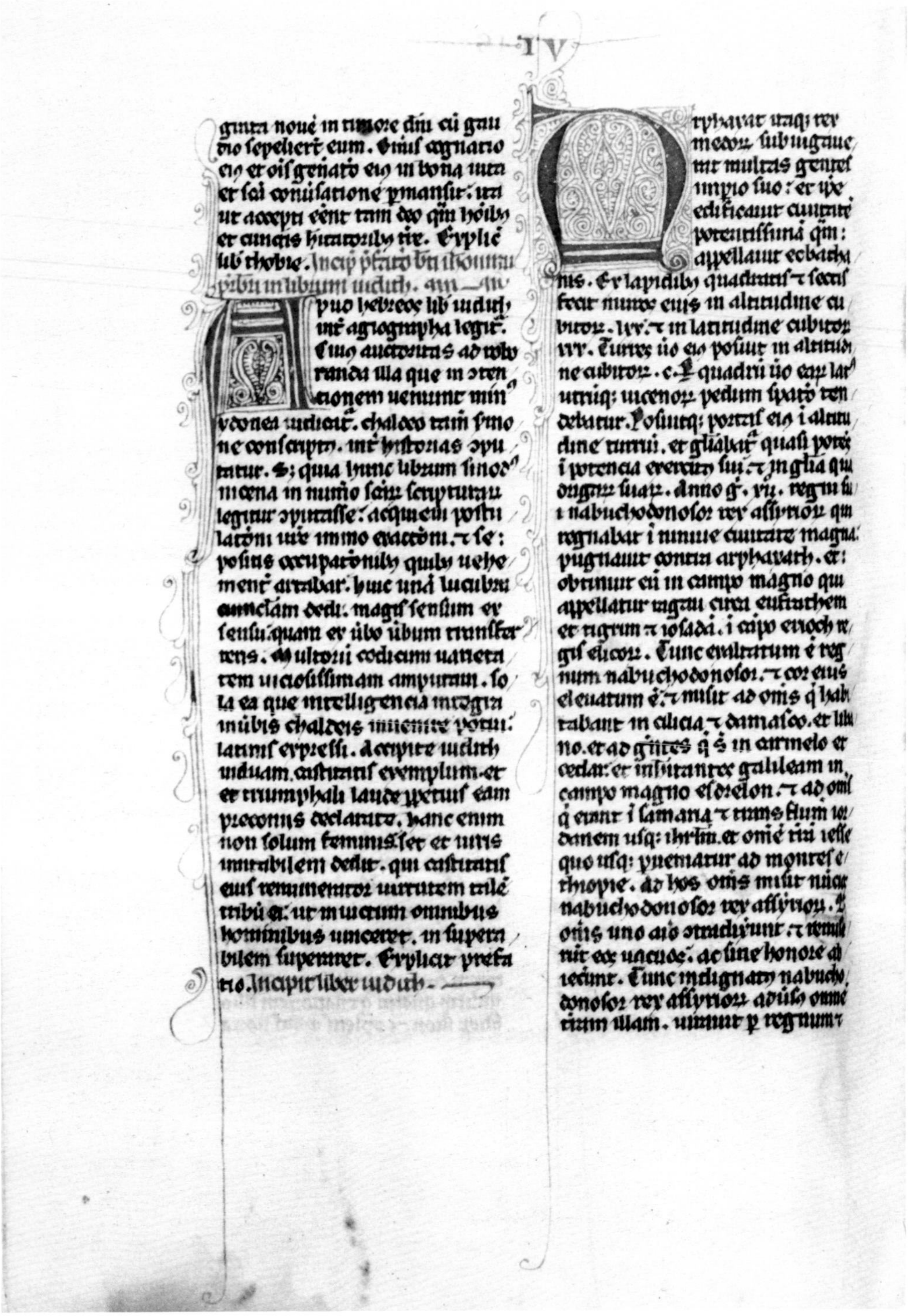

40 *Flourished initial. MS 589, f. 256v.*

Si largesse as couoytouz :
...ur serra aluee. Le tierue huue.
...us qe sumus
...entre en ma
...tyre de perte
...auenue cho
...se dire. A de
...maunder set
...a comence
...ment : Dune
vient pecche premierement.
De bon ou de mauueys rien :
Voluntiers le vꝰ dirray bien.
Quit qe dieu fit tut bon feseit :
Nest pas sage qe ceo ne veit.
Bon esteit dunke verreyment :
Lucifer au comencement.
Mes de li aueyt pecche nessaisee :
Pecche dunke sanz dutaunce.
De boue chose aueit comecerut :
Ceo veit bien qe resun entent.

Coment boue chose peut estre
encheisun de male chose.

Mes coment e par queu resun :
prent boue chose estre echesu.
De male chose com est pecche :
Coment peut ceo estre iuge.
Lucifer fu bon p nature :
Car il fu la dieu creature.
Mes il sen orgoileyt de sa beaute :
Qe dampne dieu li out done.
Dut de seon festre se seuera :
E sa nature tut empira.
Car sa volite qe mauueis aueyt :
Cen boue nature esteit.
En boue nate di desullante.

Qe a sey meimes fu nusaunt :
Dunt boue nature en pire dre...
Encheisun del pecche esteit.
En boue nature defaute fist :
Dunt il pecha e puis perist.
Si eu auez souent veu :
Qe dieu ad done grit vertu.
A ment home eu de beaute :
De seu, de force, e de saunte.
En tut est bons quit il est teu... :
Car ceo li ad tut done dieu.
Sa nate dunc est bon en sey :
Quit dieu la fit bien say e crey.
E puis quit p sa volunte :
Qe dieu fraunche li ad done.
En mal vsage sa biute met :
De sey en mentir sentremet.
E quit sey meimes eu mentist :
Formet pecche e perist.
Due pecche vient eu ver poer :
De bien quit si est empire.
Mauueis home p ceo claime :
Est eil qe fet mauueystes.
En ceo qe est home bon est sach... :
Mes mauueis est p sey pecche.
Dunt em peut bon mauueis...
Home qe mal fet p pecher.
Par ceo qe ay dit dune ver poe...
Qe pecche vient de bien empir...

Dun vient volunte.

...eyre mes de sa volunte :
...tient eu ore auez counte...
Dit vient dunke volunte :
Ne li ad pas dieu ceo done.
Volute fraunche done li a :
De voler le quel il vodra.

41 *Flourished initials, line-fillers, and historiated initial. MS 492, f. 16v.*

Historiated Initials

42 Beinecke MS 387

Latin Bible
("Ruskin Bible")

*England or northern France,
second quarter of the 13th century*

From the twelfth century on, Bibles contained many fine historiated initials, the picture within the letter offering the reader a summary of the text. This thirteenth-century Bible, which once belonged to John Ruskin, has an appealing combination of historiated initials interspersed with foliate initials. The latter, an example of which appears at the beginning of the introductory prologues of the First Book of Chronicles, are striking because of the delicacy of the designs on gold-leaf ground. The historiated initials are both attractive and instructive. One, depicting Adam and his descendants, has been painted in the interior of the first letter of the text. With its genealogical symbolism, it captures in a single scene the essence of the Biblical text, expressing the natural symbiosis of word and picture.

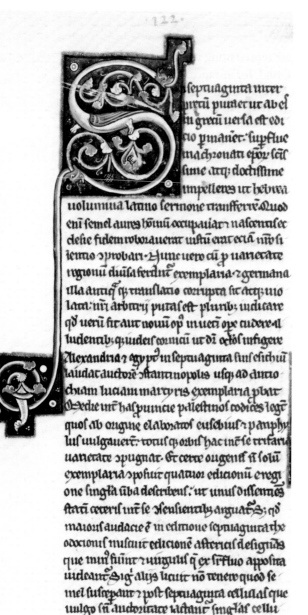

42 Left: Foliate initial. MS 387, f. 122v. Right: Historiated initial of Adam and his descendants. MS 387, f. 123r.

The decorative borders prominent in late medieval and Renaissance manuscripts grew naturally from elaborate initials. In the earliest stage of development the borders of the late thirteenth century were spiky appendages that jutted into the margins, their geometrical angularity outlining the text. By the fourteenth century the borders might run the entire length of the page.

In this fine copy of the *Divine Comedy* the historiated initial, which encloses a personification of Paradise, is overshadowed by the luxurious foliage sprouting from the letterform. Colorful borders of fleshy acanthus leaves climb up and down the space between the two columns, framing the written space. The overall dramatic effect is heightened by the liberal application of highly burnished gold leaf and the two exotic birds inhabiting the lower margin.

The borders of extravagantly illuminated manuscripts could expand to occupy most of the otherwise blank parchment. In Beinecke MS 417, a sumptuous Psalter produced in East Anglia around 1325, the borders seem to have little relationship to the historiated initials from which they grew. A scene representing the Adoration of the Three Kings before the Virgin Mary and Christ Child, for instance, is surrounded by a border of large boldly painted leaves, flowers, knots, and an assortment of grotesques, which has filled the margins. Border and initial signal a major liturgical division at Psalm 50, though the extravagance of the former has overshadowed the narrative scene within the letter.

A fine example of a fifteenth-century manuscript with purely decorative borders, this Book of Hours was produced in Bourges in the last quarter of the fifteenth

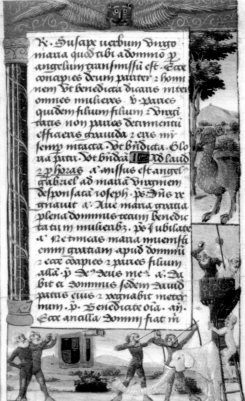

45 *Wild men at war.*
MS 436, ff. 53v–54r.

45 Beinecke MS 436
Book of Hours
("Vanderbilt Hours")
*Bourges, fourth quarter of the
15th century*

century and illuminated in the workshop of Jean and Jacquelin Montluçon, who lived in a house "at the sign of the Wild Man." Indeed, the lower margin of almost every folio of the manuscript is populated by wild men (and occasionally wild women), either hunting or engaged in warfare. On one page an elderly wild man rides a camel into combat against a younger one, who attacks with a lance. On the right a curious elephant-like creature with an exceptionally long trunk assists one group of wild men in fighting another. The borders easily drew attention away from the prayers in the text.

In addition to the many varieties of decorative initials and borders, ornamentation in finely made manuscripts often included miniatures—paintings, usually distinct from initials, that can range in size up to an entire page. In volumes illuminated for wealthy patrons, the most accomplished artists were commissioned to paint the miniatures, while less skillful or younger artists might be assigned the minor decoration. It was not uncommon in fourteenth- or fifteenth-century Paris for several artists to collaborate on a deluxe codex.

Borders and Miniatures

46 Beinecke MS 390
Book of Hours ("Savoy Hours," incomplete)
*Paris, second and third quarter
of the 14th century*

The twenty-six folios comprising this manuscript are the only known leaves to survive from the fourteenth-century Book of Hours of Blanche of Burgundy, Countess of Savoy, which was originally painted in Paris in the workshop of Jean Pucelle; additional miniatures were subsequently executed for King Charles V of France (d. 1380). On several leaves narrow bands called baguettes frame the text in the inner, outer, and lower margins. Added to the baguettes are figures such as birds, animals, hunters, and many monsters, part animal and part human. The only figure on the exhibited page directly connected to the manuscript is the woman kneeling in the lower left-hand corner, Blanche of Burgundy, the person who commissioned the volume. She gazes upward in an attitude of supplication and humility at the miniature above, in which Christ, accompanied by two angels, is tempted by the Devil. On other folios, those with miniatures and those without, a single baguette stretches along the left-hand margin of the text. The more elaborate treatment of selected borders distinguishes the important portions of the text. It is perhaps more significant that the decorative scheme has clear priority in the codex. The excellent miniatures, framed by tricolor quatrefoils and set against intricate patterned grounds, are far more remarkable than the script, which assumes a subordinate role.

47 Beinecke MS 438
Petrarch, *Trionfi*
*Florence, third quarter of the
15th century*

Beinecke MS 438 combines functional and whimsical decoration in a delightful way. This handsome copy of Petrarch's most popular work was executed in Florence in the third quarter of the fifteenth century for an unidentified "Iacopo." At the beginning of the Triumph of Love, a profile of Petrarch occupies the interior of the large introductory initial; a white vine-stem border issues from the initial into the lower, outer, and inner margins. Superimposed on the border are finely drawn animals including stag, goat, leopard, rabbit, and fox. The coat of arms painted in the lower margin, but now effaced, was supported by four frolicking putti with multicolored wings. In the upper border, which has been cropped, there appear green leafy swags and the lower extremities of five more lively putti. In addition to this historiated initial and full border is a miniature, within a gold frame, that symbolizes the main theme of the first few poems: a playful and smiling Cupid, about to shoot a flaming arrow, dominates the scene of Love Triumphant.

eus in
aduito
rium meum
intende. Do
mine ad ad
iuuandum
me festina.
lona pa
tri et filio et
fpiritui fan
cto. Sicut

erat in principio et nunc et semper et in secu
la seculorum. Amen. Alleluya. Antiene
Uenu michael pleuuime betud
Laudate pueri dominum: laudate no
men domini. Sit nomen domini be
nedictum: ex hic nunc et ufcs in seculum.
folis ortu ufcs ad ccasum: laudabile nomen
domini. Excelsus fuper omnes gentes domi
nus: et fuper celos gloria eius. Quis sicut
dominus deus noster qui in altis habitat: et hu
milia respicit in celo et in terra. Suscitans a
terra inopem: et de stercore erigens pauprem.
To collocet eum cum principibus: cum princi
pibus populi sui. Qui habitare facit sterilem: in

46 *Christ tempted by the Devil. MS 390, f. 12v.*

ELTEMPO che ri
niouia inmei solpiri
Perla dolcie memoria
di quel giorno
che fu principio a fi
lunghi martiri :

Gia ilfole al tauro luno et laltro chorno
schaldaua et la fanciulla di Titone
chorrea gielata al suo usato soggiorno.

Amor glisdegni ilpianto et la stagione
ricondocto mauieno aldriuso locho
ouogni fascio ilchor lasso ripone.

47 *Triumph of Love. MS 438, f. 3r.*

43 *Border of fleshy acanthus leaves. MS 428, f. 54r.*

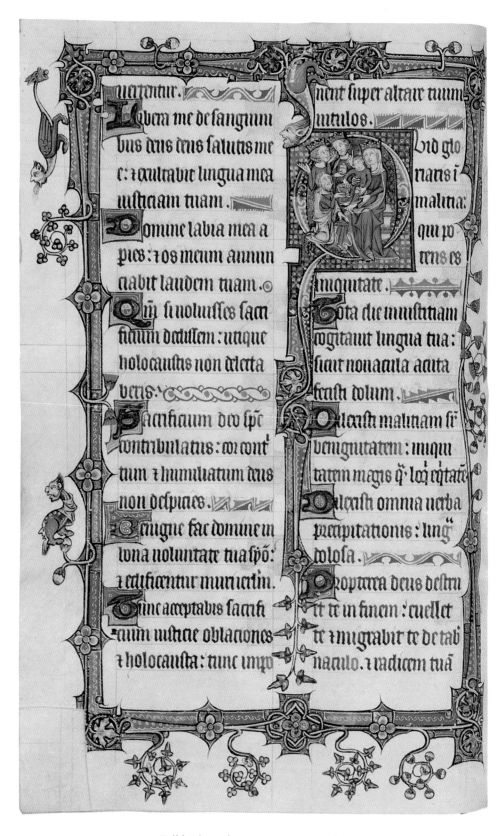

44 *Full border with grotesques. MS 417, f. 42v.*

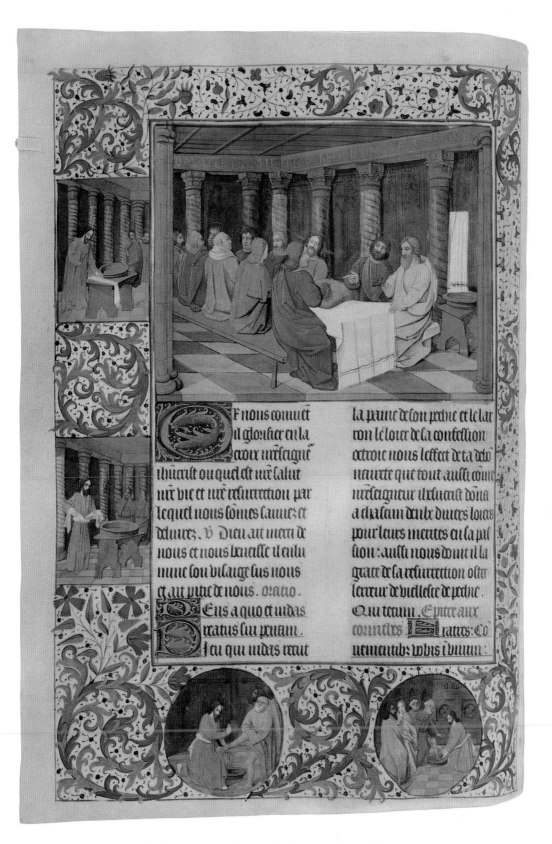

48 *Last Supper and marginal vignettes. MS 425, f. 133v.*

69 *Royal binding of King Matthias Corvinus. MS 145.*

The miniatures and borders of Beinecke MS 425 provide clarity to the text, a French translation of the Missal. The subjects of the 107 large rectangular miniatures are derived either from the daily Gospel readings or from events in the lives of the saints. Each of the miniatures is surrounded by a full border that incorporates four small marginal scenes to amplify the main illustration. The miniature which depicts Christ foretelling the treachery of his disciple Judas, as related in the Gospel according to John (13.1–30), is enhanced by subsidiary miniatures representing earlier events. In the outer margin Christ reaches for a towel and ties it around his waist. In the two roundels of the lower border Christ washes Peter's feet, then the feet of other Apostles. The integration of the large illumination with the border scenes recreates the narrative sequence of the Last Supper.

BINDING *To assemble and bind the completed manuscript was the last step in the labor intensive process of medieval book production. Unlike the roll, the codex had to be bound to be usable and durable. It was possible to keep gatherings of parchment or paper unbound as small booklets, but only when the leaves were sewn together in sequential order and protective covers were added did the codex emerge in its final form.*

During the early Middle Ages binding was probably a profession in the monasteries, distinct from the work of scribes and illuminators. In the monastery at Vivarium, the famous Roman writer and scholar Cassiodorus (ca. 485-ca. 580) displayed models of different styles of binding for the scribes to choose from: carefully transcribed texts deserved handsome covers. With the rise of universities and commercial centers in the thirteenth century, professional binders were apparently connected with particular book dealers. A manuscript might be copied in one location, decorated at a second, and bound in yet a third. When the humanists' passion for manuscripts increased book production in the fifteenth century, binders were well established, with guilds of their own. In most codices from the Middle Ages the scribes left clues that helped both themselves and the binder to arrange the gatherings in the proper order. There were several ways that scribes "signed" the quires. The simplest and probably the earliest method was to write the appropriate Roman numeral at the end of each gathering in the lower margin; in many Greek manuscripts, on the other hand, the copyists preferred to number quires on the first leaf rather than on the last. As early as the tenth century many manuscripts in Spain exhibit an alternative system: the first word or phrase of the next quire was written on the final folio of the preceding one. This use of "catchwords" prevailed into the Renaissance. Catchwords could be written horizontally or vertically, or even diagonally; they could be plain or adorned, depending upon the inclination of the scribe or the practice of a given scriptorium or workshop.

In Beinecke MS 493, an English manuscript from the third quarter of the fifteenth century, the scribe's fastidious care for the presentation of the text extended to the neatly decorated catchwords enclosed in brown and/or red scrolls. The lower right corners of many leaves also have letters of the alphabet that identify the gatherings (*a* for the first gathering, *b* for the second, and so forth), while the accompanying Roman numerals indicate the sequence of the leaves within the gathering. This shorthand method of designating both quire and leaf on the recto of a folio was carried over into early printed books.

48 Beinecke MS 425
Missal (in French)

*France (Bourges?),
third quarter of the 15th century*

Color plate, p. 51.

*Catchwords and
Signatures*

49 Beinecke MS 493
Thomas Hoccleve,
Regiment of Princes, and
other poems; John Lydgate,
Dance of Macabre

*England, third quarter of the
15th century*

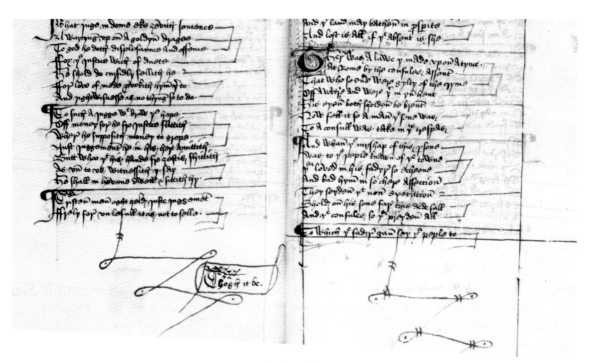

49 *Decorated catchwords.*
MS 493, ff. 97v–98r.

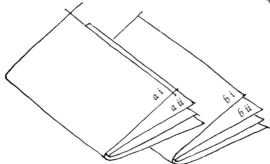

Gatherings with quire
and leaf signatures.

50 *Simple leather wrapper.*
Arabic MS 321.

After the gatherings had been placed in the correct order, the binder sewed them together; unlike the average modern binding, little or no adhesive was used on the spine of the book during the Middle Ages. Occasional holes in papyrus fragments allow us tentatively to reconstruct the earliest sewing of quire make-ups. The simplest was "stab sewing" for single leaves or several folded leaves, in which sewing occurs through the closed leaves near the spine edge. Stabbed bindings must have looked very much like wooden writing tablets linked together. For single quires, sewing through the fold of the opened book block was used, making the book easier to open. The fourth-century books found at Nag Hammadi on the Nile in 1945 were mostly single gatherings of leaves, some "tacketed" (sewn through the fold of the sheets and the cover at the same time) to leather wrappers similar to that of Arabic MS 321. The wrapper that protects this text is uncomplicated in construction and unadorned.

For more than one gathering of leaves a more complex type of "chain stitching" was used. Ethiopic MS 5 was produced later than the Middle Ages, yet its sewing is probably very like the early chain stitching of Egyptian (largely Coptic) multiple quire manuscripts, since the art of book production remained relatively unchanged in Ethiopia until at least the nineteenth century. It is thought that early European binding techniques derive ultimately from Egyptian models. The earliest surviving European binding, the Stonyhurst Gospel that was buried with Saint Cuthbert in 694 and found among his relics more than four hundred years later, is chain stitched or "Coptic sewn." In this technique no cords are used to fasten the quires together, the continuous sewing thread being the sole support. The Coptic Missal exhibits a decidedly early pattern of sewing combined with board attachment inside the back cover, although the manuscript itself is late—fifteenth or sixteenth century. The plain goatskin sides that protect the paper leaves were added at the same time that the quires were stitched together.

51 *Chain stitching. Ethiopic MS 5.*

Chain stitching.

53 *Sewing supports in a 15th-century binding. MS 4.*

Sewing Supports

53 Beinecke MS 4
St. Antoninus,
Confessionale (incomplete)
Italy, end of the 15th century

Simple chain-stitch sewing became obsolete in Europe for most books in the Middle Ages because of the size and weight of parchment codices, especially those with wooden boards. Instead, the quires were sewn to straps or thongs that were laced into the wooden boards. The earliest extant example of this technique was bound in the mid-eighth century. As can be observed in Beinecke MS 4, a small codex on which the spine is exposed, the sewing supports are thick, tawed skin straps, slit lengthwise to allow two rows of stitches. Supports could also be composed of double, twisted tawed skin or vegetable fiber thongs. When the sewing was completed, the supports extended on each side of the spine ready for attaching to the boards. Bookworms have eaten away most of the dark brown leather that once protected both the spine and covers, exposing the construction of the volume.

Chevron Pattern

54 Beinecke MS 494
Brut Chronicle (in English)
England, first quarter of the 15th century

An alternative sewing pattern is illustrated by this Middle English copy of the *Brut Chronicle* bound toward the end of the fifteenth century. The thread backtracks to catch the stitches of the previous quire, forming a chevron design. At every sewing station along the spine, the caught-up stitches fasten the gathering to its neighbor, as well as to the support. Although the sewing of the chevron patterns is neatly executed on this manuscript, the binding on the whole looks primitive.

Boards, or covers, of the medieval book were frequently of beech or oak, with oak more prevalent in northern European countries. After the wood was cut to the approximate size of the volume, the boards were shaped by bevelling the spine edge and cambering or chamfering the three outer edges to give them a less clumsy appearance. The boards were then ready to be placed above and below the text block. In order to attach the covers, channels or grooves were cut, gouged, or even burned out to accommodate the sewing supports. These grooves frequently took a

54 *Chevron design in sewing pattern. MS 494.*

circuitous path through the boards, a measure apparently intended to prevent the straps from slipping out. Early binders did not comprehend that the weakest parts of a binding were in the hinges and joints, where the boards pivot when the book is opened and closed, and not in the actual attachment of the straps.

In Marston MS 24, an early twelfth-century codex from Italy, the light parchment binding has only four pigskin straps holding the quires together: one each at the top and bottom of the spine (concealed by the turn-ins) and two near the center. The straps were laced in and out of the spine lining that is held in place by the turn-ins of the parchment cover.

The volume of English legal statutes, bound in the fifteenth century, has thongs inserted through tunnels in the edges of wooden boards. The weight of the covers and the number and size of the gatherings necessitated multiple sewing supports. When the twisted thongs reappeared on the inside of the boards, they were fitted into V-shaped grooves and fastened with wooden pegs, only one of which remains. In deluxe manuscripts the channels were filled with gesso or a similar substance to hold the straps in place and to provide a smooth surface for the covering material.

A much more common type of board attachment is illustrated by Marston MS 247 (a collection of epistles and orations in Italian by Boccaccio, Petrarch, Stefano Porcari, Filelfo, Giannozzo Manetti, Bernardo de' Medici, Bernard of Clairvaux, pseudo-Lentulus, and others). The binding supports were simply set in channels on the outside of the boards, where they were nailed as indicated by small rust marks inside the boards. Pegs were also used to strengthen the board attachments.

Board Attachments

55 Beinecke Marston MS 24
Joannes Cassianus, *De institutis coenobiorum* and *Collationes patrum* (selections); Ambrosius Autpertus, *Pro vitandis septem principalibus vitiis*
Italy, early 12th century

56 Yale Law School MSSG/ R 29/#32
Liber assisarum. 20–45 Edward III (1345–77) and two cases from 7 and 8 Henry IV (1405–07)
England, ca. 1450

57 Beinecke Marston MS 247
Florentine miscellany: epistles and orations
Italy, third quarter of the 15th century

55 *Parchment binding with support straps, turn-ins, and spine lining. Marston MS 24.*

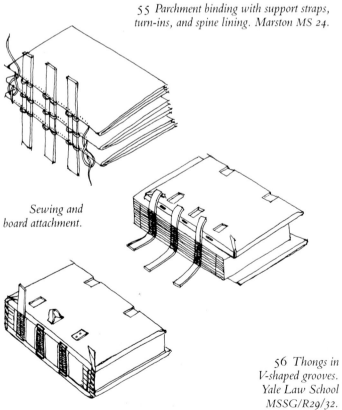

Sewing and board attachment.

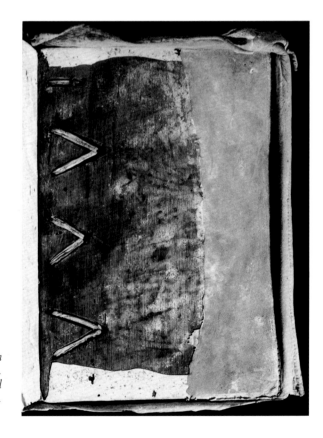

56 *Thongs in V-shaped grooves. Yale Law School MSSG/R29/32.*

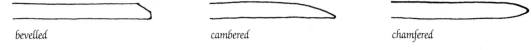

bevelled   cambered   chamfered

Shapes of boards.

Not every medieval codex had wooden boards; some covers, referred to as pasteboards, were composed of waste paper either from discarded manuscripts or, beginning in the latter part of the fifteenth century, from early printed books. It was easier and less costly to make covers from sheets of unwanted paper glued together and trimmed to the size of the codex than to shape and attach wooden boards. The increased use of paper for books also made pasteboards more feasible, since paper pages, less sensitive to changes in humidity than parchment, did not require the weight of wooden boards to keep them flat.

The leaves that constitute Beinecke MS 3, no. 34, were used in the sixteenth century to make pasteboard covers composed respectively of twelve and eleven pieces of paper, glued together and covered with leather, which is no longer present. The covers have since been dismantled in order to reconstruct and preserve fragments from a Latin and Middle English grammar handbook written in England in the fifteenth century. The holes along the inner vertical edges of the paper indicate the former location of the sewing supports; the dark discoloration around the outer border reveals where the leather cover was originally glued to the pasteboards.

Pasteboards

58   Beinecke MS 3, no. 34
Grammar handbook, in
Latin and English
(fragments)
*England, second quarter of the
15th century*

58 Pasteboards made from discarded leaves of a 15th-century paper manuscript. MS 3, no. 34.

59 *Headband and painted edges. Marston MS 141.*

Headbands and Edges

With the boards in place, the binder had to determine how to complete the binding. In some cases the spine was lined with leather or vellum, usually between the sewing supports. Headbands could be worked at this point, unless this had been done in the same operation as the sewing. Short strips, usually of twisted, tawed skin, were wound with plain thread tied down in the quires. The ends of the strips were then attached to the boards, forming small projections—the headbands—at the top and bottom of the spine. Headbands held the quires firmly in place at vulnerable points of the binding, they helped in attaching boards to the gatherings, and they enhanced the appearance of the completed volume. Colored embroidery, worked on the primary sewing, could be very elaborate and added strength to the binding, as did leather braids. The headbands on Marston MS 141, a solidly constructed codex bound in Germany in the second half of the fifteenth century, are neatly executed and sturdy.

The edges of the codex could be decorated in various ways—colored yellow or gold, or, on very fine bindings, gauffered, or tooled. Occasionally they were painted, as on Marston MS 141, where large roses appear on the paper edges.

The medieval binder usually placed a protective covering over the spine and boards. The nature of this outer layer depended upon the overall quality of the codex: options included parchment, tawed skin, leather, or fabric, and, for the so-called "treasure" bindings, precious metals, ivory carvings, and jewels. Sheepskin was a common cover material, but calf and particularly goatskin were used for more expensive bindings. The covering material was turned in around the boards and pasted down. One manuscript in this exhibition (catalogue number 56) has three layers of covering, one of which is called a chemise, with pockets into which the boards were slipped.

60 *Binding decorated with small abstract designs. Marston MS 38.*

The outer covering could be left plain for more modest volumes, or adorned through several techniques which often differed from one geographical region to another. In Italy a layout that usually consisted of concentric geometric frames was filled with impressions made by small abstract tools, mainly straight and curved rope designs and annular dots. Marston MS 38, probably a product of an Italo-Greek bindery, of which there were many in Italy after the fall of Constantinople in 1453, has a leather cover decorated in this style. The handsome brass plate, inscribed with the name of the author, is not part of the original binding, but was apparently added later in the Netherlands.

The discrete stamps found on Beinecke MS 392, a codex bound at the Carthusian house of St. Barbara's in Cologne in the second half of the fifteenth century, stand in marked contrast to the tightly articulated Italian designs. The tan calf has been carefully blind-tooled with intersecting diagonal fillets surrounded by rectangular frames. The compartments were then hand stamped with simple yet attractive patterns of roses, two-headed eagles, crowned swans, and fleurs-de-lis — binding stamps characteristic of books from this monastic library.

The panel stamp originated in the Low Countries in the thirteenth century and became especially popular in northern Europe from 1470 onward. Unlike small hand-stamping devices, panel stamps were placed with the leather covering in a mechanical press which provided more pressure. Beinecke MS 246 is a late (Bruges, ca. 1530) but nevertheless representative example of panel stamps: St. John the Baptist and Michael the Archangel are shown, separated by a row of dancing peasants.

62 *Panel stamp. MS 246.*

61 *Pictorial binding stamps: roses, fleurs-de-lis, and two-headed eagles. MS 392.*

63 *Fastening straps. Marston MS 268.*   64 *Metal bosses. MS 393.*

The final step in medieval binding was the addition of hardware. Fastenings of various sorts were needed to keep the leaves of the manuscript flat—especially parchment leaves that tend to wrinkle with changes in humidity. Such fastenings consisted of either strap and pin, the earliest and most common in northern European countries, or of a clasp and catch, with the catch usually, but not always, on the lower board in Italy and Spain, and on the upper elsewhere. Other metal fittings, such as center- and cornerpieces, were mass-produced and exported from Augsburg in the fifteenth century; many were also used in Spain and Italy, particularly on large and heavy choir books.

Fastening Straps

63   Beinecke Marston MS 268
Arnaldus, Abbot of
Bonneval, *De septem verbis
Domini in cruce*; *De laudibus
B. Mariae virginis*
Northern France, third quarter of the
12th century

From the early Middle Ages through the Renaissance contrasting colors and textures were an element of design. Marston MS 268 has a modest and presumably inexpensive binding, but it is not entirely plain. There were originally two kermes pink fastening straps, with tassels hanging from the ends. Kermes, a bright dye made from the dried bodies of certain parasitic insects, was a popular shade for medieval bindings.

65 *Chained book. Marston MS 287.*

67 *Plain student binding. Marston MS 262.*

The hardware for medieval books might also include bosses of various shapes — flowers, hearts, or flames, for example. The hat-shaped bosses on Beinecke MS 393, a codex written in Bohemia around 1423, are a remarkable feature of its plain buff-colored exterior and were added on this volume, as on many monastic books, to protect the covers from abrasion. The volume also has a contemporary parchment label on the upper cover and a title written along its lower edge — the edge that would be exposed when the book was stored flat, either in a cabinet or on a shelf.

Before the end of the thirteenth century, manuscripts had been generally stored in chests or large cupboards called armaria, *from which they were distributed to the monks and nuns for reading in the cloister or private cells. Eventually, however, special rooms for reading were established where books could be read but from which they were not to be removed — thus the origin of the chained book.*

Marston MS 287, a nicely bound volume produced at the end of the fifteenth century, has the remains of a chain hasp on its lower cover: the square metal piece originally held a metal rod to which the chain itself was attached. Since the texts in this codex were compiled for the benefit of a community of Beguines in Belgium, the book was probably bound and chained for its library.

Bosses

64 Beinecke MS 393
I. Hugh of Strasbourg,
Liber compendii (excerpts);
*Speculum humanae
salvationis*;
Statutes of Prague, etc.
II. Conrad of Brundelsheim,
Sermones de sanctis

Bohemia, ca. 1423

Chain Hasp

65 Beinecke Marston MS 287
Nichasius de Pomerio,
compiler, Life and legend
of St. Barbara, etc.

Belgium, late 15th century

Bindings were, of course, fitted to both the purpose and the purse of the prospective (or actual) owner—whether for monks, students, scholars or aristocrats. The original binding on a medieval codex can reveal much concerning the early history and provenance of the volume.

Monastic Binding

66 Beinecke MS 80

Excerpts and sermons drawn from Remigius of Auxerre, the Venerable Bede, and the early Church Fathers

Italy, first half of the 14th century

Monastic bindings were generally modest but serviceable, as befitted a religious community. Beinecke MS 80, which belonged in the sixteenth century to the convent of St. Francis at Serra San Quirico in Italy, may also have been written and bound there in the first half of the fourteenth century. Certainly the texts, excerpts and sermons by Remigius of Auxerre, the Venerable Bede, and the early Church Fathers, would suggest a monastic readership. The binding is plain, sturdy parchment over square, flush boards; a contemporary hand has briefly listed the contents of the manuscript on the lower cover.

Quarter Binding

67 Beinecke Marston MS 262

Gaspar da Verona, *Grammatica latina*

Italy, second half of the 15th century

Also at the lower end of the spectrum were the quarter bindings probably intended for students or others who did not need or could not afford more elaborate volumes. Quarter bindings had wooden boards, but only the spine and a narrow strip of the boards were protected by leather. That they were often not well executed is suggested by Marston MS 262, the Latin grammar text of Gaspar da Verona from fifteenth-century Italy. Written on paper and exhibiting only unadorned colored initials, this manuscript was presumably produced for student use and not for the aesthetic pleasure of a merchant or aristocrat.

Girdle Book

68 Beinecke MS 84

Boethius, *De consolatione philosophiae*

England? 15th century

One of the more functional styles of binding in the Middle Ages was the so-called "girdle book"—a book with a binding designed for travel. One end of the covering held the codex, carefully cradled in pockets and stitched into place, while the other end terminated in a large Turk's-head knot which could be slipped under one's belt. The book is upside down in the wrapper so that Boethius' treatise *On the Consolation of Philosophy* could be lifted and read without being detached from the reader's belt. Whether the owner of the manuscript was walking or riding on his horse, the volume was always close at hand. Only a small number of such bindings have survived.

A King's Binding

69 Beinecke MS 145

Tacitus, *Annales* 11–16 and *Historiae* 1–5 ("Corvinus Tacitus")

Italy or Buda, ca. 1475

Color plate, p. 52.

In direct contrast to the simpler medieval bindings is this magnificent volume of Tacitus written, illuminated, and bound for King Matthias Corvinus of Hungary (1410–90). An ardent bibliophile, he was concerned with preservation: his books were housed on finely carved lectern-style bookshelves, with gold-embroidered curtains to keep out the dust—a notion far in advance of his time. Regrettably, his palace library at Buda was sacked some years after his death, and most of his manuscript collection perished. Beinecke MS 145, one of the few volumes that has survived the centuries intact, is a fine example of a fifteenth-century goatskin binding, with an Oriental exuberance of flowers and leaves, the crow of the Corvinus arms set within a blue enameled shield, and a profusion of annular dots added to the basic Italian panel format composed of interlacing rope designs.

68 *Girdle book. MS 84.*

Anthropomorphic clasp.

The hand-produced codices of the Middle Ages assumed different formats depending upon their contents and upon the institutions or persons for whom they were intended. Styles of writing, decoration, and binding popular in one century or geographical location would have been inappropriate at a different time or place. Both fashion and use influenced medieval book production—from the quality of the support material and proportions of the page to the accuracy of the text.

EARLY MONASTIC BOOK PRODUCTION *In the early Middle Ages book production was centered in the monasteries. Monks copied a wide range of devotional works for their own use or for the use of missionaries. The texts most frequently transcribed were the Bible (in the Latin Vulgate translation of St. Jerome because few Western scholars could read Hebrew or Greek) and the numerous treatises, sermons, and commentaries of the early Church Fathers.*

In many monasteries scribes and artists worked in a special area, called a scriptorium ("place for writing"), and often there was a division of labor. One person or group of people would cut and prepare the parchment, while others ruled the leaves and copied the text. In a less ambitious operation, a single monk might work on every aspect of the codex, except perhaps its final assembling and binding. The scriptorium of a prosperous monastery, such as St. Gall in Switzerland or Monte Cassino in Italy, was able to provide the monastic library with most of the texts necessary for the spiritual life of the community. If a manuscript became obsolete or damaged, the parchment might be reused as a palimpsest or relegated to a scrap heap to be recycled as the pastedowns and flyleaves in the binding of other books.

Manuscripts did not always remain in the monastery that produced them. They were borrowed to be read or copied, and sometimes not returned, remaining for centuries in another abbey or convent. The physical characteristics of manuscripts often betray their place of origin—the layout of the folios, the arrangement of the prickings, the preparation of the parchment, and the ruling of the leaves all provide clues. On the basis of overall format and style of writing, three early fragments in the Beinecke collection can be assigned to specific scriptoria.

An English Volume for Missionaries

70 Beinecke MS 516
St. Gregory the Great,
Moralia in Iob, 18.41–42
(fragment)
Wearmouth-Jarrow, late 7th or early 8th century

Beinecke MS 516, a splendid fragment of Gregory the Great's monumental *Moralia in Iob*, was once part of a book probably used by missionaries. The uncial script is of the type common to the Northumbrian monasteries of Wearmouth and Jarrow during the abbacy of Ceolfrid (690–716). Located in the far northeastern corner of England, Wearmouth-Jarrow transcribed many impressive copies of the Bible and Church Fathers in the uncial script preferred in the seventh and eighth centuries for religious texts. The formal uncial of this fragment is characterized by the fine articulation of its shaded strokes and the fork-shaped serifs on the letters *C, E, F, L, S,* and *T*. The script is closely patterned on Roman models, with its neat calligraphy and close attention to detail. It is only during the second half of the eighth century, with an escalating demand for manuscripts, that the scriptorium resorted to the more quickly written local minuscule.

While MS 516 was produced in Wearmouth-Jarrow, it had found its way to Germany by the fourteenth century, when the folio served as the flyleaf in a volume owned by a monk of the Dominican convent at Soest in Westphalia. On the upper right edge of the verso, in brown ink, is his ownership inscription: "liber iste est fratris reyneri de capella. orate pro eo." (This is the book of brother Reynerus de

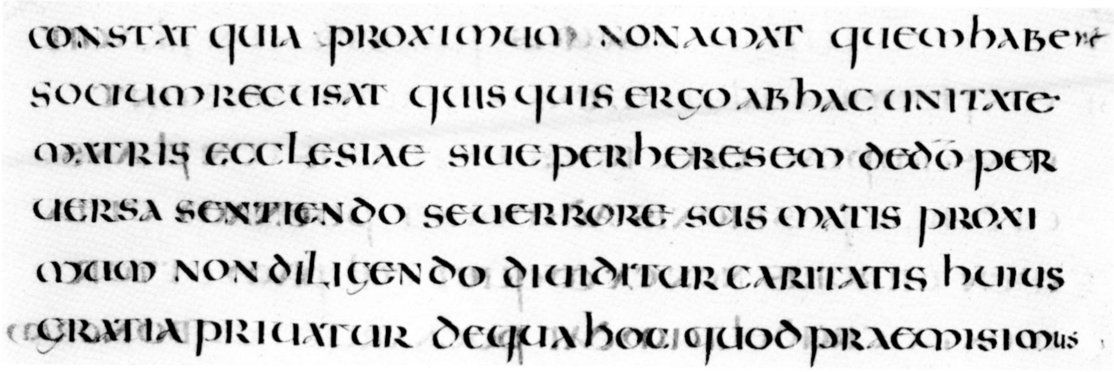

CONSTAT QUIA PROXIMUM NON AMAT QUEM HABET
SOCIUM RECUSAT QUIS QUIS ERGO AB HAC UNITATE
MATRIS ECCLESIAE SIUE PERHERESEM DEDO PER
UERSA SENTIENDO SEUERRORE SCIS MATIS PROXI
MUM NON DILIGENDO DICIDITUR CARITATIS HUIUS
GRATIA PRIUATUR DEQUA HOC QUOD PRAEMISIMUS

70 *Gregory's* MORALIA *from Wearmouth-Jarrow (fragment).*

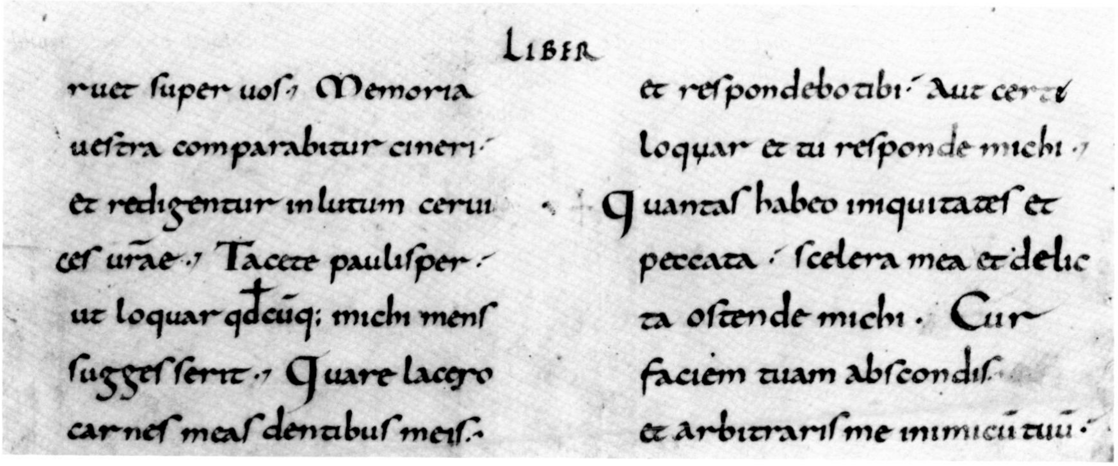

LIBER

ruet super uos; Memoria
uestra comparabitur cineri;
et redigentur in lutum cerui
ces urae.; Tacete paulisper.
ut loquar qdcuq; michi mens
suggesserit.; Quare lacero
carnes meas dentibus meis.

et respondebo tibi. Aut cert
loquar et tu responde michi;
Quantas habeo imquitates et
peccata. scelera mea et delic
ta ostende michi. Cur
faciem tuam abscondis.
et arbitraris me inimicu tuu;

71 *Carolingian Bible from Tours (fragment).*

et sermoni quem dix ihs. Cu autem et hieruso
lymis in pascha in die festo. multi crediderunt
in nomine ei uidentes signa eius que faciebat.
pse aut ihr ne credebat semetipsum eis. eo qd
ipse nosset omns. Et quia opus ei non erat.
ut quis testimonium phiberet de homine. Ipse
enim sciebat. quid esset in homine.
LECTION EXODI. In diebus illis
oqutus e dns ad morsen dics. Descende
demonte. quia peccauit ptr tuus quem
eduxisti de terra aegypti. Recesser ergo

lxvii

72 *Lectionary from Freising (fragment).*

Capella. Pray for him.) Since the works of Gregory the Great were among the most popular texts transported by missionaries, it is not surprising that the manuscript wandered far from its English homeland, perhaps with insular missionaries such as St. Boniface (675–754). Styles of calligraphy migrated with the brothers and the books they carried: the Anglo-Saxon and Irish missionaries brought both their religion and their scripts to continental Europe. By the fourteenth century, however, the uncial script of MS 516 was old-fashioned, if not unreadable—thus, its presumed dismemberment for scrap.

A Bible from Tours

71 Beinecke MS 481, Box 1, no. 5

Book of Job: 12.16–22, 13.1–7, 11–17, 22–27 (fragment)

Tours, second quarter of the 9th century

The next fragment, written at the monastery of St. Martin's at Tours in the second quarter of the ninth century, preserves portions of the Book of Job. Under the auspices of Alcuin, abbot of Tours from 796–804 and advisor to Charlemagne, the monastery had emerged as an important center of both classical and ecclesiastical learning. The uncrowded, elegant Carolingian minuscule script displayed on this partial leaf eloquently demonstrates why the scriptorium at Tours was a leading center of Bible production. The text is spaciously arranged on the leaf, there are few ligatures or abbreviations, and the letters are well formed.

A South German Lectionary

72 Beinecke MS 482, Box 1, no. 3

Lectionary (fragment)

Freising, third quarter of the 9th century

The third fragment was written at Freising in southern Germany in a script typical of manuscripts copied at the time of Bishop Anno (845–75). Long flourishes are added to the letter *m* when it occurs at the end of a line, and a similar flourish occurs on the crossbar of *e*. Many of the tall letters (*d, g, h,* for example) display thick finishing strokes at the tops of their ascenders. Other leaves that appear to be from the same mutilated Lectionary are preserved in Munich.

In both classical antiquity and the Middle Ages, texts were frequently produced to be read aloud to an audience. Early Greek civilization depended on recitation: since literature in Greece preceded the ability to read and write, the early stories of the Trojan War circulated as oral compositions before the Iliad *and* Odyssey *were written down.*

As soon as the Greek alphabet evolved from the Phoenician, Greek authors began to commit their works to writing; yet the custom of reading aloud persisted, flourishing in the Roman Empire and during the Middle Ages. Early Christians were accustomed to hearing Mass and listening to sermons; indeed, until the general spread of literacy in the twelfth century, few people could read the Latin Bible, the daily office, or the classical texts that had managed to survive the transition from roll to codex. And since books and writing paraphernalia were expensive, early medieval education emphasized oral instruction—the reading and memorization of selected texts.

The Saints Aloud

73 Beinecke MS 625

Vitae sanctorum

Spain, fourth quarter of the 12th century

Beinecke MS 625, a compilation of the saints' lives popular in the Iberian peninsula during the Middle Ages, belongs to medieval oral tradition. Produced in Spain, probably at Toledo, in the last quarter of the twelfth century, the codex consists of 106 spacious leaves of stiff and mottled parchment, each folio measuring approximately 21 by 15 inches. Since there are two columns of text with only thirty-eight lines per column, the script is large and easily legible, even from some distance. This

qui nichil possit iuuare ꝓmit ne
nichil uoluit. Matue aut surgés
abiit ad digressꝰ bestie. ⁊ fixit ge
nua in tᵃa depᵉcans dñm. ⁊ tunc be
stia eum ingenti impetu ueniut
sup eum cepit. tetruniꝭ flatib’ ac
sibilis stridonibꝫ ꝓmissis. At ille
nichil metuens: comuersus ad dra
chonem dicit. f irmat te xⱷs fili’
dei. qui pempturus é cetum ma
gnum. ⁊ ubi hec semoꝛ dixit:
statim diriſſim’ dracho omⁱs suiſ
cum spū euomens uenenum cre
puit medius. ⁊ um aut ueniſſet
finitimi habitatoꝛes ⁊ facti miᵃ
culo obstupescerent. fetoꝛis uehemᵉ
ciam nó ferentes. congregaueriut
sup eum harene moles immensas.

A stante tam ibidem patre amone.
quia nec sic quidem cum mortua
fuiſſ; bestia sine ipso ꝗpinquare
audebant. Incipit de scͦ copre.

E at quidam pᵇr in
ipsa heremo habens
monasteriū copres
nomine uir ses anno
ciuit septuaginta ⁊ ipse mⁱtas
uirtutes faciens. langueoꝛes curás.
et efficiens sanitates. f; et demones
fugans ⁊ mⁱta mirabilia faciés.
ex quib’ nó nulla etiam nr̄i ꝓsen
cia effecit. his ꝗ eum uidiſſ; nos
et osculo salutaſſet. atꝗ ex moꝛe
post oꝛonem etiam pedes lauiſſet.
requirebat ex nob qᷓ gererent in
scͦ. Nos aut rogabam’ eum ut
ipse magis nob de suis gestis ahᷘ
narraret. ex quib’ actib’ quib’ ur

ex meruis dñs ei tantam grā̄m con
tuliſſ; exponeret. At ille nichil de
dignat’ et sue uite et pimoꝛ suoꝛ
narrare nob hoꝛdinem cepit. quos
tam longe illustrioꝛes fuiſſe ꝓhibe
bant. seꝗ ipsoꝛ ꝓaritia ux exem
pla sectari. Dicebat ꝗ nichil magⁱ
m é̄ filioli. qd in nob uidet ad con
parationem scͦꝛ patrum. Erat eni
quidam ante nos uir nomine par
temutius nobiliſſim’. hic fuit pᵉr
in hoc loco monachus hac heremo
uiam salutis omnib’ nob pᵐ’
ostendit. hic aut pimo gentilis
fuit. ⁊ ationum maxim’ et sepul
croꝛ uiolatoꝛ. atꝗ in omnib’ flagi
ciis oppinatiſſim’. At quem tali
ex modo occasio salutis aduenit.

N octe quadam ad domum cuiuſ
dam uirginis deo sacrate expoli
andi grā̄ perexit. Cumꝗ machini
quibꝫdam de huiusmodi artificieb’
nocte sunt dom’ eius tecta cons
cendiſſet. querens quali arte ut
quo aditu ad penetrabilia ei’ irre
pet difficultate ꝑpetrandi opis.
innexus plurimum noctis inte
diis poſt’ sine ullo transegit ef
fectus. Poſt mⁱtos uero animi cona
tus frustra aditibꝰ ueluti feſſus
continuo sompno opprimit’ ⁊ ꝑ mᵗ
sum assiſtere sibi uidet quendam
regio habitu dicentem. Desine iᵃ
ab his ineys et ab effusione huma
ni sanguinis ceſſa. atꝗ ab exsecra
bilib’ furtis ad laboꝛem religiosū
conuerte ingulias ⁊ suscipe cele
stem angelicamꝗ militiam. atꝗ

73 *Copres narrates the life of Patermuth. MS 625, f. 12v.*

format suggests that the manuscript was not intended for an individual's silent meditation, but for oral recitation. Often while the monks were dining in the refectory, one person would read aloud a text appropriate for the spiritual inspiration and edification of the community.

Among the tales contained in the manuscript is that of Patermuth, as told by Copres. A picture of Copres shows him narrating the story of this first monk of the region. Patermuth, a notorious criminal, attempted one night to ravish a holy virgin but, frustrated in his efforts, fell asleep and had a dream commanding him to give up his sinful life. Patermuth awakened, went to church, repented, and retired to an ascetic life in the desert where he performed miraculous deeds and virtuously prepared the dead for burial.

BOOKS FOR THE DIVINE OFFICE AND MASS *A significant percentage of codices from the Middle Ages were produced for the Mass or the Divine Office. While the Mass was celebrated on specific occasions, the eight parts of the Divine Office were said throughout the day, emphasizing continual prayer and dialogue between God and man. The next two manuscripts were written for liturgical use. Both are small in size and easy to carry about.*

Two Liturgical Manuscripts

74 Beinecke MS 41
Breviary, *pars aestivalis*, use of Carmelites
Mainz, early 15th century

75 Beinecke MS 205
Processional, use of Dominicans (partly in German)
Nuremberg, ca. 1440

Since a Breviary included all the services of the Divine Office for the whole Church calendar, it was often divided into two volumes so that the manuscript would be less awkward to hold while praying. The "Winter Part" covered Advent through Easter; the "Summer Part," as exemplified by Beinecke MS 41, contained services for the remainder of the year. Though of modest appearance, this manuscript played a fundamental role in the daily religious life of its owner.

Beinecke MS 205 is a copy of a Processional specifically made for use in a Dominican house of nuns. The medieval Processional was the liturgical book containing chants, rubrics, and collects for communal processions, usually for the purpose of penitence and invocation. The codex is compact enough to be carried with ease while the woman holding it sang the music written inside. A lengthy inscription on the verso of the original front flyleaf supplies details concerning the possessor of the manuscript. Sister Barbara Pfinczingen was born in 1425 and in 1441, at the age of sixteen, entered the famous Dominican cloister of St. Katherine in Nuremberg, becoming one of its scribes. The nunnery, which dates from 1295, possessed two extensive libraries, one for standard reference works and commentaries, the other (to which this codex presumably belonged) for the nuns' personal use.

A Bulky Missal

76 Beinecke Marston MS 213
Missal
Austria, third quarter of the 13th century

In contrast to portable devotional books are liturgical manuscripts intended to be read either at the altar by the priest performing the Mass or by a choir singing hymns for the Mass or Divine Office. Beinecke Marston MS 213 is a fine example of a thirteenth-century Austrian Missal of bold and bulky format.

Decoration in Missals was generally limited to one or two miniatures depicting the death and resurrection of Christ. Marston 213 has an imposing three-quarter page miniature of the Crucifixion in which Christ hangs on a "living cross" created from the Tree of Life. The painting, added between the Preface and the Credo, enhances the Mass at the point of transubstantiation.

74 *Carmelite Breviary from Mainz. MS 41, ff. 7v–8r.*

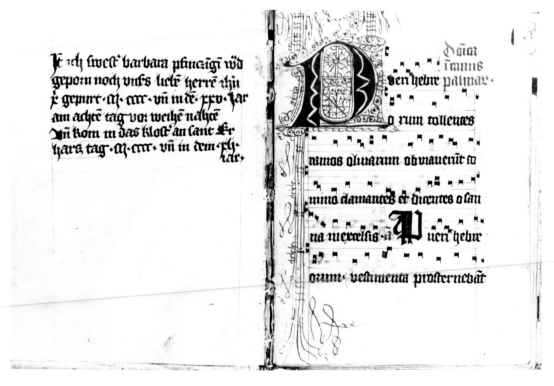

75 *Processional from a Dominican house of nuns. MS 205, ff. i verso–1r.*

mtm tubeas deprecamur. supplici confessione dice

S anctus-Sanctus-Sanctus- ces.
Domini deus Sabaoth-plem sut celi æ ter
ra gla tua. Osanna inexcelsis. Benedictus qui
uenit innoie dni. Osanna inexcelsis. ....

76 *Austrian Missal. Marston MS 213, f. 60r.*

While the Missal contains all of the Mass, the Gradual has only the parts sung by the choir. It was often a cumbersome volume, or set of volumes, with the text and music executed boldly enough for the entire choir to read. Beinecke MS 42, representative of this category of large liturgical manuscripts, weighs an astonishing 48 pounds 5½ ounces, each leaf measuring 27 by 17½ inches. Produced in Italy in the second half of the fifteenth century, the Gradual is superbly written and decorated, even the minor work being of exceptional quality. Elaborate pen-work initials incorporate intricate combinations of illusionistic jewel studs, fruit and floral borders, and swirling ivy swags.

On one page of this codex is the offset impression from a lost leaf with an extravagantly decorated border and historiated initial for the office of St. Felicitas, suggesting the book was commissioned by the church and convent of that saint in Florence. The missing leaf, apparently removed from the volume at the end of the nineteenth century, was recently identified in a private collection; the illumination of the leaf has been attributed to the hand of the celebrated Florentine artist Attavante (1452–1520/5). The initial marking the Introit for the Mass depicts St. Felicitas enthroned and surrounded by her seven sons, all holding the palm branch of martyrdom. According to legend, Felicitas and her sons were arrested as Christians. One son was beaten to death with whips, two were killed with clubs, a fourth was thrown from a cliff, and the other three were beheaded. Felicitas herself died by the sword shortly thereafter. In the foreground of the scene, two Benedictine nuns kneel before their patron saint. A full border (with eight small miniatures) gracefully surrounds the text and the music to be sung by the choir.

BIBLES *The mostly widely read book in the Middle Ages was the Bible. In comparison with the average modern Bible, the medieval Bible was a complex production, with several possible physical formats and a range of scenes to illustrate the text.*

A preference for large Bibles, often made in sets of four or five bound volumes, was characteristic of the eleventh and twelfth centuries and continued in some parts of Europe into the latter half of the thirteenth century. Beinecke MS 604 belongs to this tradition of lectern Bibles; its large pages (15½ x 10½ inches) were probably designed to be read aloud. It is a spectacular manuscript on well-prepared parchment with spacious margins and carefully executed illumination. Several folios bear the notation *lectus et correctus*, suggesting that there was considerable effort to insure the accuracy of the text. After a portion of the text was transcribed, another person, perhaps the head scribe, supplied omissions and corrected mistakes by erasing and rewriting.

On the basis of the decoration and layout of the volume, the codex can be attributed to the "Vie de Saint Denis" atelier in Paris in the middle of the thirteenth century. For the opening of the Book of Genesis, the artist has created a vertical narrative sequence of the six stages of the Creation, followed by God the Father at rest on the seventh day and the Virgin Mary holding the Christ Child.

77 Beinecke MS 42
Gradual
Florence, second half of the 15th century

78 Beinecke MS 604
Latin Bible; Stephen Langton, *Interpretationes nominum hebreorum*
Paris, mid-13th century

77 *Florentine Gradual. MS 42, f. 126v.*

Missing leaf from MS 42, now in the private collection of Jean Preston.

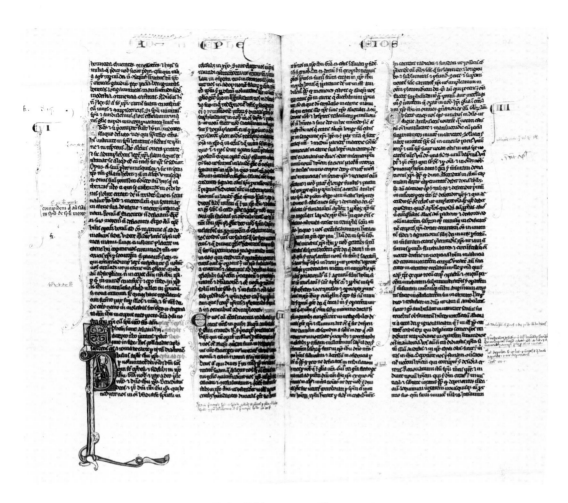

79 *Pocket Bible. MS 433, ff. 377v–378r.*

In contrast to the lectern Bible, the leaves of Beinecke MS 433 are tissue thin, the script extraordinarily tiny and compressed. The codex measures a mere 7½ by 5 inches. The illumination, by virtue of its small size, lacks the monumental quality observed in a lectern-style Bible. The smaller codex exemplifies the dramatic change in the production of Bibles that took place in Paris at the turn of the thirteenth century—a change that may be attributed to the increased emphasis on teaching the Bible in the university and among the members of the newly founded Dominican and Franciscan Orders. A compact one-volume Bible became essential for both student and preacher. It was important, as well, that the text be standardized. For the first time in the history of the Latin Bible, the order of the books and their names were firmly established, and under the influence of the Biblical scholar Stephen Langton (d. 1228), the books were systematically divided into the numbered chapters still used today.

To meet the increased demand, certain workshops in Paris specialized in the production of portable Bibles. Beinecke MS 433 comes from one of them, the so-called Soissons atelier, active between 1230 and 1250. The volume has been heavily used—its parchment is often crumbled and discolored and several readers

Pocket Bible

79   Beinecke MS 433
Latin Bible ("Vanderbilt Bible"); Stephen Langton, *Interpretationes nominum hebreorum*; list of readings
Paris, second quarter of the 13th century

have added marginalia. A fifteenth-century inscription states that the Bible was given to the Dominican convent of St. Andrew in Faenza (Italy) by Father Vincent de Albicellis, who had purchased it with money from his parents. Two centuries after its production, Beinecke MS 433 was still in use, neither its text nor its format outdated.

PRIVATE DEVOTIONAL TEXTS *In the thirteenth century, the Hours of the Blessed Virgin Mary were combined with other devotional material, including psalms, to form the genre called the Book of Hours, which gradually superseded the Psalter as a manual for private prayer. Its purpose was to evoke the assistance of the Virgin through personal celebration of the Divine Office. Like the pocket Bible of the thirteenth century, the Book of Hours was a "best-seller" of the late Middle Ages and Renaissance. The Hours of the Virgin were arranged according to the canonical hours of the day with illustrations or miniatures to complement the text. A typical sequence of illuminations might include the Annunciation for matins, the Visitation for lauds, the Nativity for prime, the Annunciation to the Shepherds for terce, the Adoration of the Magi for sext, the Presentation of Christ in the Temple for none, the Flight into Egypt for vespers, and the Coronation of the Virgin for compline.*

Early Book of Hours

80 Beinecke MS 657
Book of Hours
*Metz, second quarter of the
14th century*

This beautifully preserved Book of Hours originated in the second quarter of the fourteenth century at Metz in Alsace-Lorraine on the border of France and Germany. The idiosyncratic illuminations from this workshop differ significantly from the standard repertoire of scenes prevalent in the following century. The Psalms of Penitence (6, 31, 37, 50, 101, 129, 142 in the Roman Catholic enumeration), a standard feature of Books of Hours in the fourteenth century, begin on folio 83r in MS 657; the oblong miniature at the bottom of the preceding page appears to be an overgrown line filler added to occupy the lower portion of the written space. Yet the subject matter, the Arma Christi (the emblems of Christ's Passion), is well suited to the Penitential Psalms. The objects employed to torture Christ before and during his Crucifixion—scourge, nails of the cross, sharpened lance, pincers, and hammer— are graphically depicted against a background of impeccably tooled gold leaf.

The principal miniature at the beginning of Psalm 6, representing the Last Judgment, shows Christ sitting on a rainbow with the Virgin Mary and John the Evangelist on either side. He displays the wounds in his hands, side, and foot, which extends from underneath his robe. The full bar border incorporates a depiction of the owner of the manuscript, a woman, accompanied by a bushy-tailed animal, kneeling in prayer with her arms lifted toward Christ. In the lower border the dead arise from their graves. The small historiated initial that marks the opening word of the psalm shows the cloth used by Veronica to wipe the sweat from Christ's brow on the road to Calvary; it bears the imprint of the sorrowful face of Christ.

During the fifteenth century Books of Hours were produced in vast numbers to meet the demands of a prosperous middle class. A sumptuously decorated Book of Hours such as Beinecke MS 400 was a status symbol, coveted not only because of its religious importance, but also because it placed the owner among the socially elite.

80 *Book of Hours from Metz. MS 657, ff. 82v–83r.*

82 *The "Rothschild Canticles." MS 404, ff. 65v–66r.*

81 *"Lévis"* or *"Bedford Hours."* MS 400, f. 93r.

REGES PLVRIBVS DELECTATI
onibus gaudent: Aliis victo
ria plus placet: Aliis regimé
populorum per exibitionem
legum: Aliis plus magnorum
operum constructio: Aliis céf
satio: Aliis ueneris delectatio: Aliis thesaurorum
congregatio: Aliis benefitiorum exibitio: Aliis
ludorum & festuitatum ordinatio: Aliis plus t
uirtum & scientiarum acquisitio: Aliis uenatio:
Aliis alia: Ex omnibus uenatio uidetur magis cô
ueniens regibus & magis propria: Fere autem oés
reges ceteriq; magnates hanc preceteris appetunt

98 *Falcons at rest. MS 446, f. 1r.*

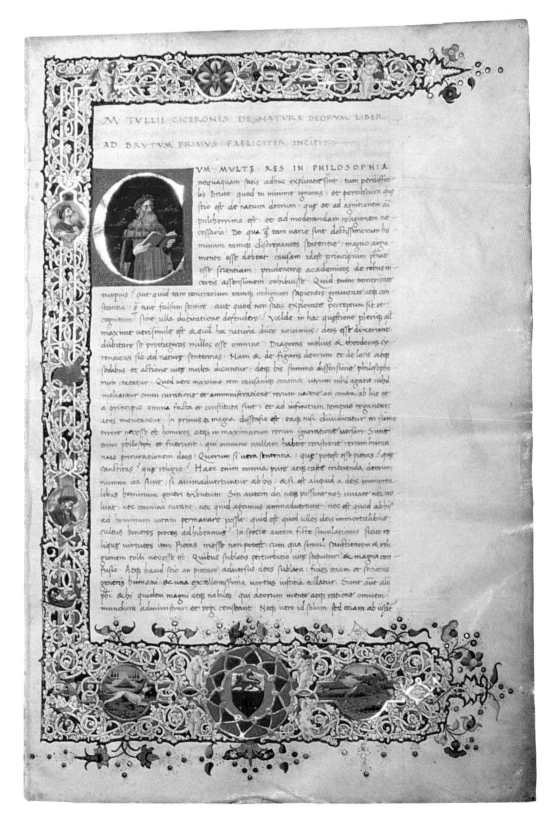

104 *Luxury volume of Cicero commissioned by János Vitéz. MS 284, f. 1r.*

Produced in Paris in the second decade of the fifteenth century, the volume represents a collaboration between two important illuminators of the period. Five of the miniatures, which have been attributed to the so-called Luçon Master, represent the latest known painting from his shop; the other eleven illuminations are some of the earliest works of the Bedford Master, who flourished between about 1410 and 1435. While its fine illuminations set it apart from the average manuscripts of a Paris atelier, the codex does contain a fair sampling of the texts found in a Book of Hours: a calendar giving the saints' days and certain other fixed feasts; four readings from the Gospels followed by two short prayers to the Virgin; the Hours of the Blessed Virgin Mary; the Penitential Psalms; a litany; the Hours of Christ's Passion; the Short Hours of the Cross; the Short Hours of the Holy Spirit; the Office of the Dead; several prayers (in French); a selection of suffrages of particular saints; and finally, a number of votive Masses.

The painting that depicts Christ's betrayal is the finest miniature by the Luçon Master in this manuscript. The brightness of the shimmering gold contrasts starkly with the vivid blue background and the silver of the soldiers' armor; the impact of the page is further heightened by the border of lush acanthus leaves inhabited by delicately drawn birds and angels. Unlike the small Book of Hours from Metz, the marginal decoration does not relate directly to the prayers.

Not all medieval religious texts can be neatly categorized as Breviaries, Bibles, or Books of Hours. Beinecke MS 404 is unique in the composite nature of its text and the unusual iconography of its illuminations. Commonly known as the "Rothschild Canticles," the manuscript was produced around 1300 in northern France, probably in the diocese of Thérouanne. The first part of the volume contains verbal and artistic metaphors intended to inspire meditations upon the reader's anticipated vision of Christ. Along the lower edge of the full-page miniature on folio 66r, the bride (*Sponsa*), traditionally identified with the Church, is languishing in bed meditating on her love for God. (One portion of the accompanying text quotes the Song of Songs, "Sustain me with raisins, refresh me with apples; for I am sick with love. O that his left hand were under my head, and his right hand embraced me!") Christ, the bridegroom, looks out from behind the rays of the sun and extends his hand down to the woman at the moment of her contemplative ecstasy.

The second part of the manuscript is a patchwork of texts, most of which were extracted from the wisdom books of the Bible. One passage gives a short but detailed account of monstrous races, associating physical abnormality with moral degeneration. Each of the small framed miniatures depicts a deformity, including one man with a single large foot and another with hooves of a horse instead of feet.

Although the codex became the dominant format for texts after the fourth century, the roll assumed a number of particular functions. Prayer or indulgence rolls of small format were popular in the fourteenth and fifteenth centuries, particularly in England. Few have survived, since they were carried about without the solid protection provided to a codex by its covers. Beinecke MS 410 measures more than five feet in length and contains several prayers, each portion surrounded by lively and colorful drawings to enhance the reader's spiritual experience. The scroll opens with a short

Parisian Book of Hours

81 Beinecke MS 400
Book of Hours ("Lévis or Bedford Hours")
Paris, ca. 1410–20

The Rothschild Canticles

82 Beinecke MS 404
Composite devotional book
Northern France, late 13th or early 14th century

Indulgences for 32 Millennia

83 Beinecke MS 410
Prayer roll (in Latin and English)
England, fourth quarter of the 15th century

poem on Christ's physical suffering and a list of prayers to be recited for an indulgence of 32,055 years:

O man unkynde
Bere in thy mynde   My paynes smerte
And thu shall fynde
Me treu and kynde   Lo here my herte
The pardon for v pater noster. v aves and a credo
Whyth pytuusly beholdynge the armes of cristis passyon is
xxxii m. and lv. yeres.

Immediately preceding the text is the full-length figure of Christ standing with his arm around the Cross, flanked by the emblems of the Passion. A variation of the same scene follows after the text, but with emblems bigger and bolder. The three nails of the Crucifixion, more than six inches in length, dominate the miniature, together with the bloodied hands, feet, and heart of Christ.

The marked increase in lay piety in fourteenth- and fifteenth-century England resulted in the production of a large number of manuscripts with devotional texts appealing to a bourgeois audience. John Lydgate (1370?–1451?), a monk of Bury St. Edmunds, was one of the most prolific writers of works of popular piety. Although modern readers have been critical of his poetry, citing lack of imagination and tedious length, in the fifteenth century Lydgate's works circulated widely both in manuscript copies and in the early printed versions of Caxton, Wynkyn de Worde, and Pynson. His Lyf of Our Lady *is extant in almost fifty manuscripts as well as in Caxton's edition of 1484 and Redman's of 1531.*

Two Lydgates

84 Beinecke MS 281
John Lydgate,
Lyf of Our Lady
Southern England, ca. 1470

85 Beinecke MS 660
John Lydgate, *Lyf of Our Lady*; *Privity of the Passion*
England, fourth quarter of the 15th century

Two fifteenth-century manuscript copies of this work tell us something about Lydgate's audience. Beinecke MS 281 is an elegant codex, probably produced in southern England around 1470. The text is neatly written in a formal style of English bookhand characterized by delicately decorated ascenders and descenders along the upper and lower edges of the written space; illuminated initials and borders occur at the beginning of Books 1–4. This is a deluxe manuscript commissioned by the wealthy patron whose heraldic devices appear on two pages. A large coat of arms in a green, orange, and gold frame faces a smaller set in the lower margin. Dogs of noble appearance accompany both devices, the arms of the Carent family from Dorset and Somerset.

Beinecke MS 660, produced in the last quarter of the fifteenth century for an individual of modest circumstances, stands in sharp contrast. It was written on parchment of inferior quality, with many flaws and irregularities. The scribe has tried to crowd the text, sometimes squeezing as many as forty-one lines on a page. There is no ornamentation, not even the simplest heading in red, though the copyist left space for small decorative letters at the beginnings of chapters. This modest codex was probably written by or for a cleric for his own use; a second devotional text, the late fourteenth-century *Privity of the Passion*, has been added at the end of the volume. The two copies show that Lydgate's *Lyf of Our Lady* appealed to a wide and varied readership, from a wealthy gentry family to an anonymous reader for whom an unadorned text may have been all that was financially feasible.

86 *Biblical scenes*
from Petrus Comestor's
HISTORIA SCHOLASTICA.
MS 674, f. 1v.

83 *Indulgence roll.*
MS 410.

84 *Deluxe copy of Lydgate's* LYF OF OUR LADY. *MS 281, ff. 5v–6r.*

SECULAR AND VERNACULAR TEXTS *The rapid growth of universities at the end of the twelfth century and beginning of the thirteenth and an overall increase in literacy had far reaching repercussions in the book trade. There was, generally speaking, a greater demand for texts—secular texts in vernacular languages as well as religious and devotional works. Students, scholars, aristocrats, merchants, educated men and women all required books, more books than could be produced by monasteries alone. To meet the demands of the broader learning, secular workshops, such as those in the university environments of Paris, Oxford, and Bologna, came into being.*

The flourishing interest in learning and the increase of reading for pleasure among the middle classes went hand in hand with a marked growth in literacy not only in Latin but also in the vernacular languages of Europe. Latin was the language of the Church, the law, and most literature in the Middle Ages, but toward the end of the period authors such as Petrarch, Chaucer, and Christine de Pizan chose to write in their native tongues and to compose poetry and prose that appealed to a secular audience. During the course of the fourteenth century many works of classical antiquity, such as Livy's Roman History *and Aristotle's* Ethics, *were translated into French and other national languages to satisfy the demand for vernacular reading material by the well-to-do laity.*

Several handsome manuscripts from the Beinecke collection illustrate one aspect of the new

87 *God creates Eve from Adam. MS 129, vol. 1, f. 8v.*

secular literature, its fascination with the historical and legendary past. The people of the Middle Ages loved history in all of its manifestations, from the genealogical lists of the Old Testament to the travels of Alexander the Great. Tales that in preceding centuries had been recited by wandering minstrels were now committed to parchment for the enjoyment of a literate clientele.

Bible stories were an important part of the curriculum of the new universities and provided a basis for many widely read vernacular texts. Composed between 1169 and 1173 by "Peter the Eater," the *Historica scholastica* is an exegetical commentary on the historical books of the Bible, but when the Bible did not provide sufficiently detailed information, the author felt free to supplement the text with passages from the Church Fathers and pagan authors. Because of its witty and anecdotal style, this compendium was eagerly read by students, monks, and nuns in the late Middle Ages and was frequently translated into the vernacular languages of Europe. In Paris it was a standard university textbook during the lifetime of its author and for generations thereafter.

Beinecke MS 674 is an early manuscript of the *Historia scholastica*, produced soon

Bible Anecdotes

86 Beinecke MS 674

Petrus Comestor,
Historia scholastica

Belgium, fourth quarter of the 12th century

after the author's death. On the basis of its decoration the codex has tentatively been assigned to the Benedictine monastery of St. Remaclus at Stavelot in southern Belgium. It is a large, handsome volume, carefully copied by three or four scribes. The spaciousness of the leaves and the impressive *In Principio* ("in the beginning") initial at the beginning of the text suggest it was an expensive manuscript.

A vernacular version of Petrus Comestor's text, Guyart Desmoulins's French rendition from the end of the thirteenth century, was extremely popular in the Middle Ages. It circulated in at least four versions during the next two centuries. In transforming the *Historia scholastica* for the secular reader, Guyart provided his audience with the full text of the Bible and the commentary on it, all in French. Beinecke MS 129, an attractively illustrated manuscript executed in Flanders in the third quarter of the fifteenth century, is textually close to the earliest version of Guyart's text.

Like the Latin Vulgate Bible, the French *Bible historiale* often had a complex program of decoration. Beinecke MS 129, composed of two volumes of 266 and 294 leaves respectively, measures approximately 17 x 13½ inches and has eighteen miniatures and seven historiated initials. The marginal glosses were tied to the commentary by symbols in an attempt (not always successful) to keep Guyart's text and commentary separate from the later additions. The paintings are closely related to the narrative. As the story of the seven days of Creation unfolds, each day is depicted in a large roundel. For the events of the sixth day the artist has shown Adam leisurely resting his head against a rock, while God is creating Eve. Many animals, including a strange looking elephant with a horse's body, inhabit the land.

Romances

Competing in popularity with the *Historia scholastica* and the *Bible historiale* were the romances devoted to chivalry and courtly love, codes which reflected the ideals of the aristocracy rather than the realities of medieval society. The adventures of King Arthur, the kingdom of Camelot, and the infidelities of the beautiful Queen Guenevere captured the imagination of the medieval audience. In the thirteenth and fourteenth centuries large, extravagantly illuminated manuscripts of such texts were commissioned by wealthy aristocrats. Beinecke MS 229, one of three volumes executed for Guillaume de Termonde (1248–1312), the second son of Gui de Dampierre, count of Flanders, contains the final third of the romance, the quest for the Holy Grail and the death of King Arthur. The miniatures and historiated initials—over 160 in all—almost allow the reader to recreate the storyline without reading the text. The script is bold yet elegant, and the decoration is lavish with gleaming gold leaf and vibrant color. A particularly fine illumination appears toward the middle of the codex. In the upper register King Henry, seated on his throne, commands Walter Map to write the story of the death of Arthur—the last segment of the romance that occupies the end of the codex. In the lower register the knights set off for a jousting tournament at Winchester.

Advice to Women

In opposition to a male-oriented view of the world were the writings of Christine de Pizan, an unusual woman who lived and wrote at the end of the fourteenth century. Born in Venice around 1364, she was educated at the French court where her father was astrologer to King Charles V. Married at fifteen and widowed at twenty-five, she turned her attention to writing both prose and poetry in French and

87   Beinecke MS 129
Guyart Desmoulins,
Bible historiale
*Flanders, third quarter of the
15th century*

88   Beinecke MS 229
Arthurian romances
(vulgate version): *Le livre
de Lancelot du Lac*, part III,
La queste del Saint Graal,
and *La mort au Roy Artus*
France, late 13th century

89   Beinecke MS 427
Christine de Pizan,
Livre des trois vertus
*Northern France, third quarter of the
15th century*

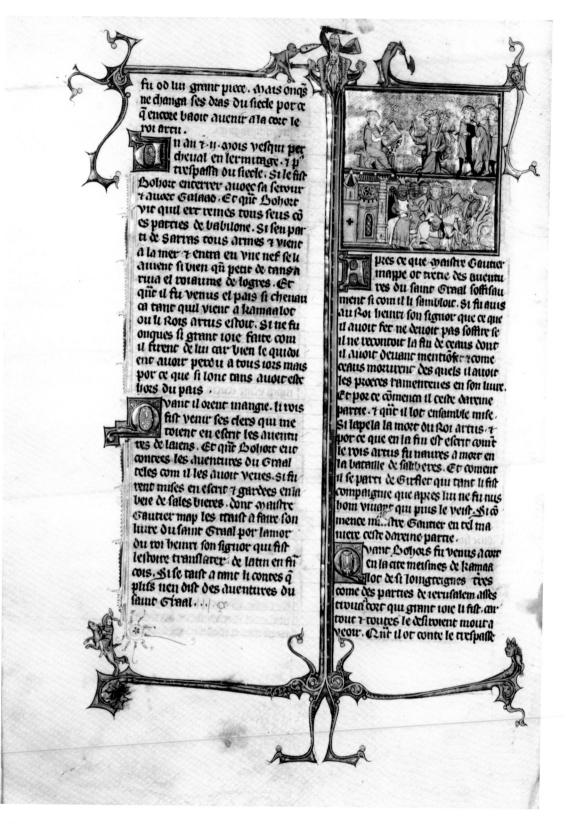

fu od lui grant piece. Mais onqs
ne changa ses dras du siecle por ce
q encore vaoir auenir ala core le
roi artu.

N an et .ii. apois vesqui per
cheual en lermitage. i p'
trspassa du siecle. Si le fist
Bohort enterrer auoec sa seour
i auoec Galaad. Et que Bohort
vit quil ert remes tous seus en
es parties de vabilone. Si sen par
ti de Sarras tous armes i viene
a la mer i entra en vne nef se li
auient si vien qn peut de tans a
ruia el roiaume de logres. Et
que il fu venus el pais si cheuau
ca tant quil vient a kamaaloc
ou li Rois artus estoit. Si ne fu
onques si grant ioie faite com
il firent de lui car vien le quidoi
ent auoir perdu a tous iors mais
por ce que si lone tans auoit este
hors du pais.

Vant il orent mangie. li rois
fist venir ses clers qui me
toient en escrit les auentu
res de laiens. Et que Bohort eut
contees les auentures du Graal
teles com il les auoit veues. Si fi
rent mises en escrit i gardees en la
vere de sales vieres. dont maistre
Gautier map les traist a faire son
liure du saint Graal por lamor
du roi henri son signor qui fist
lestoire translater de latin en frā
cois. Si se taist a tant li contes q
plus nen dist des auentures du
saint Graal.

pres ce que maistre Gautier
mappe ot tretie des auentu
res du saint Graal soffisau
ment si com il li sambloit. Si fu auis
au Roi henri son signor que ce que
il auoit fet ne deuoit pas soffire se
il ne recontoit la fin de ceaus dont
il auoit deuant mention i come
ceaus morurent des quels il auoit
les proeces ramenteues en son liure.
Et poe ce comenca il ceste darrine
partie. i que il lot ensamble mise.
Si lapela la mort du roi artus i
por ce que en la fin est escrit comt
le rois artus fu naures a mort en
la bataille de salyeres. Et coment
il se parti de Girflet qui tant li fist
compaignie que apres lui ne fu nus
hom viuans qui puis le veist. Si com
mence maistre Gautier en tel ma
niere ceste darrine partie.

Vant Bohors fu venus a cort
en la cite meismes de kamaa
loc de si loingtreignes tres
come des parties de ierusalem asses
tiuua cort qui grant ioie li fist. car
tout i toutes le desiroient moult a
veour. Quit il or conte le trspasse

88 *The life and times of King Arthur. MS 229, f. 272v.*

was able to support herself and her three children as a popular author. An early feminist, Christine disliked the image of the helpless woman projected in the medieval romances and wrote to inspire all women, not merely those of the aristocracy.

Beinecke MS 427, an elegant copy of her *Livre des trois vertus*, was produced in northern France in the third quarter of the fifteenth century. In this treatise Christine invokes the three virtues of Reason, Righteousness, and Justice to help her institute precepts and rules of conduct for women of various social stations. In one miniature the three virtues, personified as fashionably dressed women, are enthroned: Righteousness holds a sword; the central figure, Reason, gazes upon an open book; Justice holds the scales. In the foreground, women and children from the lower classes of society are seated in attendance, eager to receive advice.

Genealogy was an important part of the late medieval interest in history. Scholars attempted to produce comprehensive plans that accounted for all the major legendary and historical figures, from the Creation to their own day. The roll was the perfect format for such projects. The lines of descent could begin at the top and proceed through generation after generation uninterrupted by page breaks. A sufficient number of these large scrolls survive to indicate that they were a specialty of the fourteenth and fifteenth centuries, that they were popular in France and England, and that they were frequently written in the vernacular.

Two Genealogical Rolls

90 Beinecke Marston MS 242
Genealogical roll of the English kings (in English)
London, 1466–67

The Beinecke collection has two impressive examples of this genre. Marston MS 242, written in Middle English, was probably made in London or Westminster in a workshop that produced a considerable number of rolls similar in script, contents, general layout, and decoration. Measuring more than twenty-eight feet in length, the scroll is constructed from fifteen parchment membranes carefully glued together. Prickings down the entire length of both outer edges and faintly ruled guidelines indicate that the overall format was precisely planned and coordinated. Although it is tempting to think that this roll was executed membrane by membrane and then assembled, the fact that the gold leaf and paint were applied over the seams shows that this was perhaps not the case.

The genealogy begins with Adam and Eve and ends with Edward IV, king of England. Since only Elizabeth is named of Edward's children, the roll must have been completed between February 1466 and August 1467. Nearly everyone seems to appear in this genealogy, including quasi-historical figures like King Arthur and scores of Anglo-Saxon kings represented by rows and rows of bright crowns.

91 Beinecke Marston MS 180
Genealogical/historical roll of the Popes, the Roman emperors, and the French and English kings (in French)
France, ca. 1410–13

Marston MS 180 is wider, but shorter (only seventeen feet), than the Middle English roll. The French roll spans a broader range of genealogy, encompassing four discrete but related strands of European history. The first column (on the left) presents the Popes from Christ to Alexander V (whose term lasted only from June 1409 to May 1410), though the accompanying diagram incorporates his successor, the anti-Pope John XXIII. The second column is devoted to a chronology of Roman emperors, starting with Augustus and ending with Louis of Bavaria, the Holy Roman emperor in 1328. The third column, which expands along the lower portion to fill the entire width of the roll, traces the French monarchy back to the foundation of Venice by Trojan nobles and concludes with the reign of Charles VI, king of France

89 *Reason, Righteousness, and Justice speak to an audience of women. MS 427, f. 72r.*

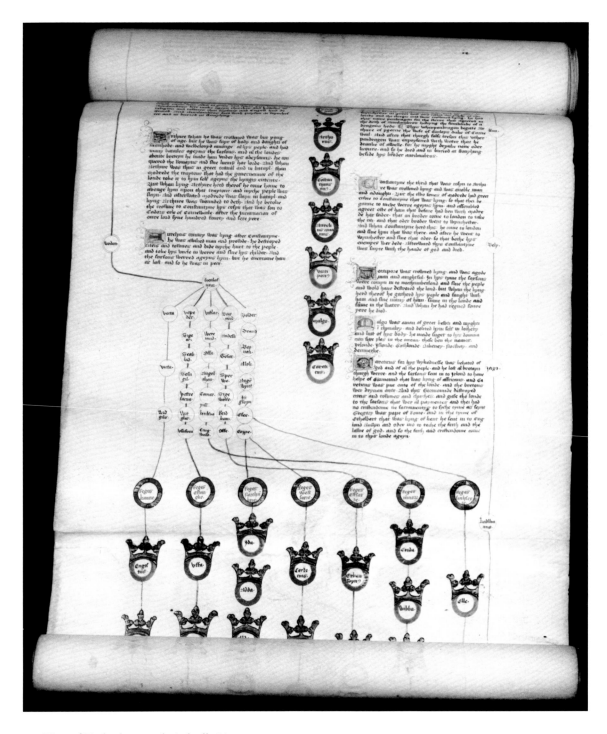

90 *Kings of England: a genealogical roll. Marston MS 242.*

from 1380 to 1422. The kings of England occupy the final column on the right, ending with Henry IV, who died in 1413.

Although both the text and the linear arrangement of the diagrams in this roll emphasize the major figures of legend and history, the decoration depicts cities and

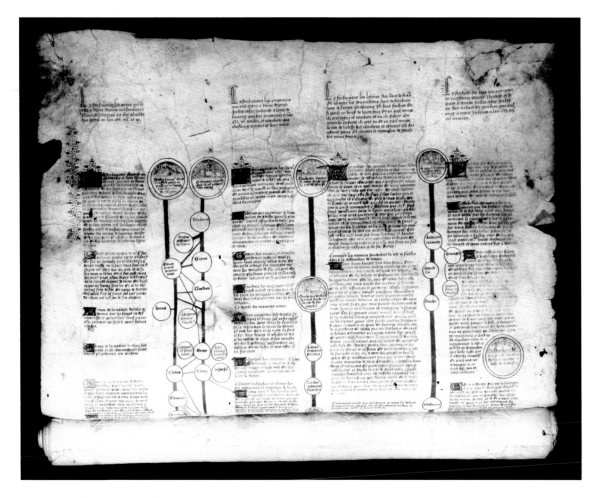

91 *History of Europe, in roll format. Marston MS 180.*

churches thought to have been founded under particular rulers. As might be expected, the majority of the decorative roundels apply to the French monarchs. All of the architectural drawings represent buildings that look late medieval, even if supposedly built by the Romans or the early English kings.

During the Middle Ages the four primary areas for study were the arts (rhetoric, geometry, arithmetic, logic), law, medicine, and theology. Marston MS 67 contains the text of Priscian's *Grammatica minor*, a work at the center of the medieval study of the arts. Priscian's treatise, amply supported by examples from classical Greek and Latin writers, synthesized what was known about grammar before the sixth century. The Beinecke copy is a schoolbook of very modest appearance that was used and annotated by several generations of students. The letters in the outer margins of most leaves, placed there by the original scribe, provide easy reference, the initials standing for classical authors (*v* for Vergil, *t* for Terence, *ho* for Horace). The main script suggests that the volume was written in eastern France in the final third or quarter of the twelfth century; the dense marginal glosses were added in the

Student Texts

92 Beinecke Marston MS 67
Priscian, *Grammatica minor*

Eastern France, fourth quarter of the 12th century

92 *Annotated grammar text. Marston MS 67, ff. 9v–10r.*

second half of the following century. As in schoolbooks everywhere, there are mindless doodles, notes, and drawings.

This particular schooltext once belonged to Jacques de Vitry (ca. 1170–1240), historian, preacher, and participant in the Fifth Crusade, who says in an ownership inscription that he purchased the volume for 32 denarii. Vitry was both a student and master in Paris, where he bought the volume, probably secondhand, since his own inscription is written over an extensive erasure. Not only could a student commission handsome new codices from Parisian bookdealers, he might also find a serviceable used book.

93 Yale Medical Historical
MS 12
Aristotle, *Opera varia*,
Latin tr.
*Paris, third quarter of the
13th century*

The many works of Aristotle were a staple in the literary diet of Parisian scholars. Aristotle's method of close analysis and argumentation appealed to an age when theologians could dispute endlessly on whether the angels moved the heavens. In 1255 the faculty of arts in Paris established requirements for the study of Aristotle's works, and this manuscript, which is attributed to Paris in the third quarter of the thirteenth century, includes all except one of the mandatory works. The parchment used in this codex is finely prepared, and the script, a neat Gothic bookhand, is written in a narrowly defined central space. The remainder of each page has been designated to receive the ample marginal annotations, including diagrams. Historiated initials mark the beginnings of each of the twelve treatises, while smaller decorative letters indicate internal divisions. (In two places crude drawings, faintly outlined in lead, occur next to the historiated initial, intended to provide guidance

93 *Works of Aristotle for the university student. Yale Medical Historical MS 12, f. 261r.*

for the illuminator.) At the top of each leaf running headlines appear in red and blue. The spacious margins and the attractive relationship between text, commentary, and ornamentation contrast with the cluttered appearance of the well-thumbed Priscian manuscript.

STATIONERS AND THE UNIVERSITIES *Faced with the increasing demand for inexpensive books and accurate texts, the bookdealers in university towns developed the* pecia *or piece system, probably beginning in the mid-thirteenth century. In Paris, the location for which there is the most extensive evidence, the* pecia *system operated under the auspices of special bookdealers, or university stationers, who owned copies of the textbooks required in the curriculum. These copies were divided into pieces, each of which was numbered separately and could be rented out to individuals who needed an exemplar from which to copy the text. Several scholars could copy from one complete text at the same time, speeding up production. The system also attempted to guarantee the purity of the text, since each new copy was a direct descendant of the stationer's "fair" copy. A committee of university teachers monitored the stationers' exemplars annually and posted a list of approved texts available from each.*

Pecia Notations

94 Beinecke MS 207
St. Thomas Aquinas, *In tertium librum Sententiarum Petri Lombardi*
Paris, ca. 1270

Beinecke MS 207, a copy of the commentary of the Dominican St. Thomas Aquinas (1225–74) on the *Sentences* of Peter Lombard, was produced in Paris around 1270 by means of the *pecia* system. As recently demonstrated, the manuscript was transcribed from a copy vended by William of Sens (Gulielmus Senonensis), a stationer on the rue St. Jacques, where the Dominican house of studies was also located. William of Sens was from a family of stationers who were active from about 1270 to 1342 and played a fundamental role in the dissemination of the works of St. Thomas Aquinas. Beinecke MS 207 contains some *pecia* notations along the lower edges of the leaves where the scribe recorded the number of the stationer's piece just finished, although most of the marks were undoubtedly trimmed when the codex was bound. The volume also contains an unusual statement by the scribe: "Nota confundatur stacionarius qui me fecit deturpari librum alicuius probi uiri" (Take note! Confound the stationer who made me disfigure the book of some worthy man.) Something obviously went amiss, for there are extensive erasures in the manuscript where the curse appears. On the basis of internal evidence it appears that Thomas Aquinas may have revised a portion of the work after he had turned it over to the stationer. The stationer then required the scribe to incorporate those revisions into a part of the text that had already been copied. The manuscript may therefore be more accurate textually, but the need to scrape off the old passages and superimpose the revisions offended the sensibilities of a scribe who took pride in the neatness of his work.

Corrected and Signed

95 Beinecke MS 338
Guido da Baysio, *Rosarium decretorum, secunda pars*
Bologna, first half of the 14th century

While Paris was producing the works of Aristotle, Thomas Aquinas, and other prominent scholastic thinkers, the bookdealers in Bologna were issuing bulky volumes of civil and canon law for students all over Europe.

Beinecke MS 338, a fine example of a Bolognese manuscript executed in the first half of the fourteenth century, contains the commentary of Guido da Baysio on the Decretals, the official laws of the Church. Guido da Baysio studied in Bologna and was appointed archdeacon there in 1295; he became a professor at the university in

94 *Comments by an irate scribe. MS 207, f. 46r.*

95 *Corrector's notes in a Bolognese canon law text. MS 338, f. 45r.*

1301 shortly after completing the commentary transcribed in this codex. His treatises on canon law were an essential component of the curriculum. The elegantly written and illuminated volume shows evidence of having been copied in pieces and then carefully corrected. In the margin of the page exhibited is the outline of a small four-leaf clover inscribed with the name of the corrector ("ray" for Raimondo or Rainerio?), the number of the *pecia* ("24"), and the fact that the text was corrected after being transcribed. Each piece of the codex is signed.

COMMONPLACE BOOKS *Not every medieval manuscript had a single text or a thematically coherent series of texts. Some heterogeneous collections were compiled and written by individuals for their own use. The name "commonplace book" is applied to this sort of manuscript.*

The Book of a French Officer

96 Beinecke MS 648
Commonplace book: letters, verses, writings on chivalric offices and heraldry, etc., by Jean Faucket

Burgundy, late 15th or early 16th century

This commonplace book belonged to Jean Faucket (or Faucquet), King of Arms of Philip, Duke of Burgundy, and a hero of the Battle of St. Omer, who, as a result of his loyalty to the Emperor Maximilian I, was commended, knighted, and given a pension. His manuscript was probably written sometime after 1497, the latest date to appear on its pages. Faucket was the court official responsible for planning state occasions, including tourneys, coronations, and funerals. Among many other miscellaneous items, the book contains his copious writings on chivalric offices, copies of testimonial letters given to him by the emperor, his own verses composed along courtly models, and a treatise describing how the office of the King of Arms originated in France. Several times the proud owner signed his name or added his monogram with calligraphic flourishes. The volume may have been compiled over several years, existing in three or four independent sections before being bound together and covered in elegant black silk.

The longest segment of the manuscript is a work on heraldry including more than four hundred and forty brightly colored coats of arms, primarily of families from France and Flanders, but also of kings around the world. The largest, encompassing a full page, is that of Jean Faucket, the arms granted to him by the emperor. Although this commonplace book is not likely to be praised by scholars for artistic merit, it reveals much about the interests of a prominent French nobleman at the end of the age of chivalry.

A Book for All Seasons

97 Beinecke MS 163
Commonplace book ("Wagstaff Miscellany"): texts in Latin and English, probably compiled by John Whittocksmead

England, mid-15th century (part 1) and 14th century (part 2)

Another commonplace book provides a glimpse into the life of an English gentleman, probably John Whittocksmead (1410–82), a member of Parliament for constituencies in Somerset and Wiltshire, whose surname appears at the conclusion of several works. Unpretentious in appearance, the codex is composed of many texts, short and long.

In Latin he included a *History of the Seven Wise Men of Rome*, a parliamentary text, and a copy of Giordano Ruffo's *Diseases of Horses*, as well as a selection of prayers, poems, and prognostications. In Middle English he incorporated wide-ranging scientific and practical texts. More than twenty leaves contain culinary recipes, 189 in all, frequently for the preparation of wild game and fish, since hunting and fishing were popular sports for the English upper classes. There are directions for "Stewyd

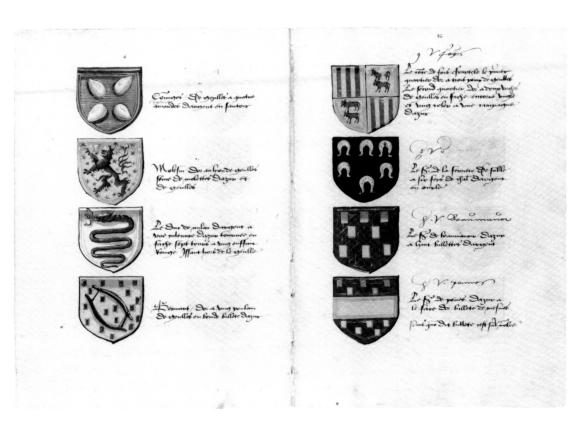

96 *Coats of arms. MS 648, ff. 11v–12r.*

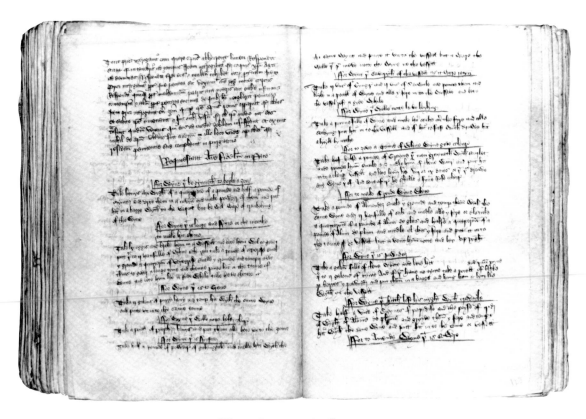

97 *Wine recipes. MS 163, ff. 122v–123r.*

pertrych," "Pyke in sauce," "Salmon roasted in sauce," "Perche boyled," and "Chykens in bruett" (chickens in broth). Four pages of wine recipes, thoroughly unappetizing, advise the reader what to do "For Wyne that saveryth of the vessell as it Were rotyn," "For Wyne that Wolle notte hold colour," "For to make reede Wyne White." There is a text in this book for virtually every contingency—medical prescriptions for ailing animals, a poem on hawking, a short treatise on astronomy, a charm against thieves.

HANDBOOKS *During the Middle Ages and Renaissance numerous handbooks imparted specialized information to nonspecialists—handbooks commissioned and read by people who had the time and financial resources for such activities as hunting, fishing, and astrology.*

Three Treatises on Falconry

98 Beinecke MS 446
Moamin, *De scientia venandi per aves*, Latin tr. Theodore of Antioch; Dancus rex and Guillelmus falconarius, falconry treatises

Naples, third quarter of the 15th century
Color plate, p. 83.

Whether game was pursued directly (venery) or with birds of prey (falconry), hunting was the primary outdoor leisure activity of the Middle Ages. Because of the popularity of falconry there were numerous medieval handbooks on the care and training of these birds. Beinecke MS 446, a splendidly written and illuminated codex originally owned by Ferdinand II of Aragon, preserves three treatises on the topic. The works are attributed to Moamin (who originally composed in Arabic), Dancus Rex (King Dancus), and Guillelmus falconarius (William the falconer). Moamin was apparently an Arab falconer whose treatise was translated into Latin by Theodore of Antioch, a philosopher and doctor at the court of Frederick II of Hohenstaufen (1194–1250) in Sicily. Dancus is reputed to have been a medieval king of Armenia whose work heavily influenced William the falconer, the son of another falconer from Naples.

At the beginning of the Beinecke manuscript there is a splendid miniature of five falcons relaxing in their palatial abode with hoods over their eyes, as if to keep them from darting away from the falconer at an inopportune moment. The unidentified artist has added an unexpected element of realism, delicately painted bird droppings below the perch.

A Manual of the Horse

99 Beinecke MS 454
Drawings on matters equestrian; Manuel Díaz, *Libre de cavalls*
Spain, second half of the 15th century

Throughout the Middle Ages the horse was indispensable for agriculture, transportation, warfare, and sport. Some breeds, especially those from Spain, were prized for speed and agility, others for large size and endurance in battle, where they might have to carry a knight wearing five hundred pounds of armor. The horse, which contributed to the rapid spread of Islam through northern Africa and across Spain, participated in almost every major land battle of the Middle Ages. The influence of Arabian horses on the Spanish breeds was of great importance when Ferdinand and Isabella reunited the Iberian peninsula under Christianity and when the Spanish explorers reintroduced horses into the New World.

Beinecke MS 454 is devoted to horses. Produced in Spain in the second half of the fifteenth century, the volume opens with three full-page drawings showing the anatomical parts of the horse, the best sites for blood-letting, and which signs of the zodiac affect which parts of the animal. Sixty-five diagrams of bits follow, some of them with explanations of their construction and use. The final and longest portion of the codex contains the treatise *Libre de cavalls* (The Book of Horses) composed by Manuel Díaz in Valencian dialect. Díaz, an official at the court of Alfonso V, king

Los signes deus escrits son contraris cascu en certa part del Cauall car quan
uoltu fer alguna cura en lo cauall deuen guardar que lo signe no sia sobre
aquel locs que uolren fer la cura.// Aries es contrari al cap.// Taurg al
coll.// Cancer als pits.// Geminis als brahons.// Capricorng als genols
Pias als peus e ales mans.// Scaurpig als botons.// Aquarg ales cames.// Sa
gitarg ales cuxes.// Libra ales anques.// Leo al cor.// Virgo als buxels e
al ventre.//

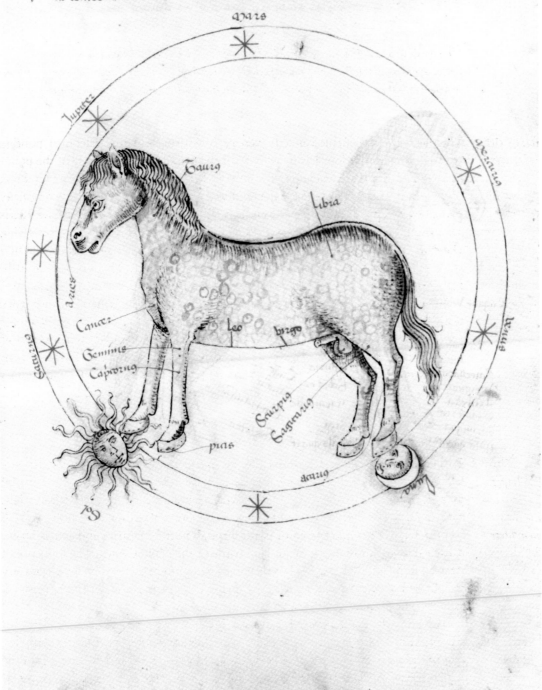

99 *Signs of the Zodiac and the horse. MS 454, f. 1r.*

100 *Instructions for making a fishing float. MS 171, f. 85v.*

of Aragon, based his work on several Italian authors whose writing he encountered after the Spanish conquest of Naples in 1435. Medieval interest in the horse knew few geographical or language barriers.

A Guide to Angling

100 Beinecke MS 171
The Treatyse of Fishing with an Angle
England, mid-15th century

Fishing was a popular sport in fifteenth-century England. There were fishponds on the grounds of most large estates and monasteries as well as on some less prosperous holdings, since the sport appealed to the lower social orders as well as to the nobility and gentry. One did not need horses, well-trained falcons, or hunting dogs to fish. The technique was sophisticated, but the individual could make his own tackle at little cost.

Beinecke MS 171, probably from the mid-fifeenth century, appears to contain the oldest text of *The Treatyse of Fishing with an Angle*, first printed by Wynkyn de Worde in 1496. In contrast to the books on falconry and horses, this volume is modest, even homely, in appearance. The treatise is written on paper of average quality in an uneven script with no decoration. The frequent errors may be the result of the scribe's ignorance of the subject matter, but it is clear from the condition of the manuscript that it did not sit on the shelf unread.

The prologue, asserting that angling is the "menys and cause to reduse a man to a mery spryte," answers the fifteenth-century debate as to which sport was the most noble. While the hunter returns home at the end of the day sore and sweaty, his clothes torn and some of his hounds lost, the fisherman undergoes spiritual and moral revitalization and attains peace of mind.

The handbook offers a wealth of practical information to enhance the pleasure of angling: how to make a rod and color the fishing lines (including instructions for making the color green), how to determine the type of line suitable for each fish, how to make floats, and how to locate the best places for fishing. One of the more detailed discussions lists the best sorts of bait. Salmon prefer red worms at the beginning and end of the season—or worms bred in a dunghill. Trout, on the other hand, described as "a dainty fish," will only respond to certain bait in particular months—in March a minnow, in July the little red worm and codworm together. For a serious fisherman in fifteenth-century England this text would have been indispensable.

The final handbook is one of the world's most mysterious manuscripts, a collection of unidentified texts in an unidentified language in unbroken cipher. Despite numerous attempts by scholars and cryptographers to crack the code, the precise contents of the manuscript remain a puzzle. We do not know who wrote the text or when and where the manuscript was produced. The drawings in the volume are nearly as enigmatic as the text. Almost every leaf is filled with botanical and scientific sketches, many full-page in size, of an unsophisticated but lively nature. Structurally, the codex does not conform to the standard format encountered in most medieval books; inserted throughout are large fold-out sheets containing peculiar, often bizarre diagrams and drawings.

On the basis of the illustrations, the manuscript has been divided into sections. The astronomical or astrological portion contains twenty-five astral diagrams made up of radiating or concentric circles filled with the signs of the zodiac, stars, and inscriptions. Each page of the so-called biological section reveals small-scale drawings of pudgy female nudes. Some are swimming in ponds of blue and bilious green fluids, others emerge from objects resembling cans, tubes, or plumbing fixtures. No one has been able to explain satisfactorily the strange activities of these women. The pharmaceutical part of the codex contains more than one hundred drawings of what seem to be medicinal herbs and roots, complete with appropriate jars and vases.

The Voynich Manuscript

101 Beinecke MS 408
Scripta aenigmatica: scientific or magical text(s) in an unidentified language, in cipher
Central Europe? late 15th or first half of the 16th century

RENAISSANCE HUMANISM *Humanism, the cultural movement that began in Italy in the fourteenth century, attempted to recover the spirit and literary achievements of ancient Greece and Rome. Classical literature, in Greek and Latin and in vernacular translation, was read, taught, and celebrated. The early humanists, studying the works of Cicero, Seneca, and Juvenal, were influenced more by these classical models for poetry and rhetoric than by the scholastic writings of medieval theologians.*

Petrarch, pre-eminent among the early humanists, inspired Italian scholars to search for early manuscripts of classical literature, which had been languishing neglected in monasteries and cathedral libraries. The works of Livy, Pomponius Mela, and Propertius were all rediscovered, and to some extent edited by Petrarch during his residence at the papal curia in Avignon. The authors of the Middle Ages fell from favor as Boccaccio, Coluccio Salutati, and Poggio Bracciolini rescued Latin writers of classical antiquity. The Renaissance enthusiasm for Greek language and literature began in earnest with the visit to Florence in 1397 of Manuel Chrysoloras, a Byzantine diplomat and scholar, who taught Greek to such notable humanists as Guarino of Verona and Leonardo Bruni. The booktrade flourished, and old texts, recopied and often revised, found their way into private and public libraries. The Renaissance codices were not usually executed in the Gothic scripts and decoration of the late Middle Ages, but in

102 *Left: 12th-century text of Juvenal. MS 450, f. 1v.*
Right: 15th-century replacement leaf by an Italian humanist, f. 2r.

new styles of writing and illumination based on standards developed during the Carolingian era. Carolingian manuscripts provided not only the texts of the classical authors, but a model for the physical format of new books as well.

A Recycled Classic

102 Beinecke MS 450

Juvenal, *Saturae*,
with scholia

Central France? first quarter of the 12th century (replacement leaves, third quarter of the 15th century)

The transmission of the classical tradition from the Middle Ages to the Renaissance is attested by Beinecke MS 450, a much used copy of Juvenal's *Satires* with extensive scholia originally composed in the late eighth or ninth century. Produced in the first quarter of the twelfth century, perhaps in central France, the main text is written in a late Carolingian script in a narrow column. An ownership inscription from the fourteenth or fifteenth century in the lower margin of the first leaf shows that the manuscript was still read long after it was written. An unidentified Italian humanist subsequently replaced leaves that were damaged or missing sometime in the third quarter of the fifteenth century. The fifteenth-century insertions attempt to replicate the *mise-en-page* of the twelfth-century leaves. This manuscript of Juvenal was, in effect, recycled for reading three centuries after it was first copied.

Marston MS 7, containing four texts popular among the humanists, belongs to the transition from the Gothic period to the Renaissance. The opening portion of the volume was written in a fine humanistic bookhand, whereas the second part of the manuscript is in a script reminiscent of the Gothic hands of the fourteenth century and the writing of Coluccio Salutati. The unusual initials, which may represent an early experimental attempt to imitate Carolingian motifs, are painted in yellow, rather than gold, and are set against bright blue grounds with simple vine-stem patterns and touches of fine white filigree patterns.

The first of two distinct annotators added headings, running titles, and proper names in the margin using a neat, humanistic bookhand characterized by an exaggeratedly tall *s*. It has recently been shown that these notes were written by Guilielmino Tanaglia, a friend of Niccolò Niccoli, to whom Niccoli bequeathed part of his book collection. Lorenzo di Giovanni Tornabuoni, who owned the volume in the second half of the fifteenth century, added a two-line inscription, an ex libris in Greek and Latin, and a second set of glosses in a sprawling humanistic cursive. Tornabuoni was the cousin of Lorenzo the Magnificent and a student of Politian. Condemned for plotting the return of the Medici, he was beheaded in 1497. Other details of his life are few, although it is known that he borrowed Filelfo's copies of the *Iliad* and *Odyssey* from the Medici library in Florence. The presence of his notes reveals the movement of the book as it wandered in the inner circle of humanist scholars in fifteenth-century Italy.

While Renaissance humanism had its roots in Italy, it spread rapidly during the fifteenth century across the Alps into eastern and northern Europe. In Hungary the first humanist was János Vitéz, bishop of Nagyvárad and later archbishop of Esztergom. Vitéz, who excelled as orator and writer, was chancellor of the University of Pozsony (today Bratislava), founded by King Matthias Corvinus in 1467 on the model of the university in Bologna. In addition to advising King Corvinus on acquiring a library for the royal palace at Buda, Vitéz personally collected an array of Renaissance manuscripts.

Beinecke MS 284, a carefully crafted volume of Cicero's philosophical works, was commissioned by Vitéz, whose arms appear in the lower border of the first folio. The codex was copied in Florence in 1470 by the professional notary Piero Cennini and illuminated by Mariano del Buono. The delicately painted historiated initial contains a portrait of Cicero set against a vivid blue sky with clouds. The border decoration is composed of the white-vine scrollwork characteristic of Italian humanistic manuscripts. Every aspect of this manuscript suggests that it was intended for a connoisseur of fine books—the unblemished parchment, the generous proportions of the page, and the elegant script and decoration. Even the binding, ruby-red goatskin with foliate brass catches, is of exceptional quality.

Gutenberg's invention of printing with moveable type in the mid-fifteenth century initiated a wide-ranging technical revolution. Texts could be printed in great numbers on paper and sold for perhaps one-fifth the price commanded by handwritten codices. Since early printed books coexisted with manuscripts and used manuscript books as models, it is not surprising that the

Circulated in Florence

103 Beinecke Marston MS 7
Cicero, *Orationes Philippicae, In Catilinam*; pseudo-Sallust, *In Ciceronem*; pseudo-Cicero, *In Sallustium*
Florence, early 15th century

Book for a Connoisseur

104 Beinecke MS 284
Cicero, *Opera philosophica*
Florence, 1470
Color plate, p. 84.

·PROHEMIO·DI·IACOPO·DI·MESSER·POGGIO·ALLO·
ILLVSTRISSIMO·SIGNOR·FEDERCO·DA·MONTE·
FELTRO·CONTE·DVRBINO·NELLA·HISTORIA·
FIORENTINA·DI·MESSER·POGGIO·SVO·PADRE·ET·
TRADOCTA·DALVI·DILATINO·IN·LINGVA·FIOR
ENTINA·

·NARRANO·GLISCRIPTORI·
inuictissimo principe· che ALexandro
magno figliuolo di Philippo Re de
macedoni uenendo alsepolcro di Achille
non pote contenere lelacrime· ricorda
ndosi che inquella eta chera allora
lui auea facte molte cose degnie cohe
delle uirtu sue dipoi sera abattuto atro
uare Homero scriptore· pel quale acto
in modo parue accusassi eltempo auea·
consumato fino aquel di che mai dipoi siposo fino atanto che nō
solo supero lagloria dachille· ma diructi glialtri greci. Iulio cesa
re ancora affermano che dopo molti secoli uedendo laimagine
dalexandro saccese aoperare cose marauigliose· Ilperche se el
monumento dachille· e una uana pictura ebono tanta forza
che commouessino et constrignessino glianimi loro aoperare
cose degnie di eterna gloria· che dobiamo stimare facessi el
uedere tucto di etriomphi eleuictorie riportauano eloro cita
dini? Certamente come esacti sono dapreporre alle parole· e
quello suede congliocchi piu muoue che quello sintende da
altri· cosi lecose uegiamo fare daglhuomini prestanti molto
piu cinfiammano edestanci aexercitare optere degnie disomma
loda che quelle legiamo oudiamo. Sendo adunq proueduto
dalla natura che non possiamo uedere altro che lera nostra cisi
mostri· perindustria eingegnio deglhuomini excellenti estata
trouata lahistoria· allaquale commettendo lecose occorrono
indiuersi luoghi possiamo come inuno specchio raguardare
eprocessi deliuenti seguiti in molti secoli. Diche sipuo compre
hendere quanta utilira essa arrechi alla generatione huma
na· equanto uolendo essere grata glisia obligata· sendo sola

105 *Poggio's* HISTORIA FLORENTINA. *MS 321, f. 1r.*

PROHEMIO DI IACOPO DIMESSER POGGIO ALLO IL
LVSTRISSIMO SIGNOR . FEDERICO DA MONTE FEL
TRO CONTE DVRBINO . NELLA . HISTORIA . FIO
RENTINA.DIMESSER. POGGIO.SVO PADRE. ET TRA
DOCTA.DAL VI.DI LATINO.IN LINGVA FIORENTINA

ARRANO . GLI SCRIPTORI INVICTISSI
mo principe che ALexandro magno Figliuolo di
Philippo Re De macedoni uenendo al sepolcro di'
Achille non pote contenere le lacrime : ricordandosi
che in quella eta chera allora lui auea facte molte
cose degnie eche delle uirtu sue dipoi sera abattu
to atrouare Homero scriptore : pel quale acto imo
do parue accusassi el tempo auea consumato sino
aquel di che mai dipoi si poso sino atanto che non solo supero lagloria
dachille : ma di tucti glialtri greci. Iulio cesare ancora affermano che do
po molti secoli uedendo laimagine dalexandro saccese aoperar cose ma
rauigliose. Il pche se el monuméto dachille. e una uana pictura ebono tá
ta forza che cómouessino & cóstrigniessino gliáimi Loro aopar cose de
gne di eterna gloria : che dobiamo stimare facessi el uedere tucto di
etriomphi eleuictorie riportauano eloro cittadini : Certamente come e
facti sono dapreporre alle parole : equello si uede cógliocchi piu muoue
che quello sintende daaltri : cosi lecose uegiamo far daglhuomini prestá
ti molto piu cinfiammano edestanci aexercitare opere degnie di somma
loda : che quelle legiamo o udiamo. Sendo adunque proueduto dalla'na
tura che non possiamo uedere altro che leta nostra ci simostri : per idu
stria eingegnio deglhuomini excellenti estata trouata lahistoria : alla
quale commectendo lecose occorrono indiuersi luoghi possiamo come
inuno specchio raguardare eprocessi deuiuenti seguiti inmolti secoli
Diche si puo comprehendere quanta utilita essa arrechi alla generatio
ne humana : equanto uolendo essere grata glisia obligata : sédo sola cu
stodia fedelissima dellopere nostre equella che sempre celefaccia presen
te : Ecolsuo mezo riducendoci amemoria lopere degli huomini singula
ri ci inuiti aoperare difarci immortali epeprogressi daltri cimostri laui
ta diciascuno : ecósigli nel diliberare epartiti presi ecostumi delle repu
bliche. Leuarieta grandi della fortuna : euarii euenti delle ghuerre : accio
che colexemplo daltri possiamo eleggiere quello sia utile anoi e alla pa
tria : Imperoche cominciando dapiu antichi che giouerebbe quanto al
la fama di Nino re degli assirii. Semirami e Ciro tante guerre. tante fa
tiche tanti marauigliosi exerciti : tante prouincie subiugate etanti re uin
ti senó fussino state dagli scriptori celebrate : Che gloria sarbbe. a Solone

a.i

106 Incunable edition of the same work, based on MS 321.

earliest printed volumes closely resembled their exemplars from the Middle Ages and Renaissance. In Italy, roman and italic type fonts were based on humanistic bookhand and cursive script. Like the producers of fine manuscripts, early printers left spaces for display script and decorative initials to be filled in by rubricators and artists, or for such minor decoration as paragraph marks and pen-flourished initials.

From Manuscript to Printed Book

105 Beinecke MS 321
Poggio Bracciolini, *Historia Florentina*, Italian tr. Jacopo di Poggio

Florence, ca. 1475

106 Beinecke Zi +4243
Poggio Bracciolini, *Historia Florentina*, Italian tr. Jacopo di Poggio

Venice, Jacobus Rubeus, 8 March 1476

Among the many humanistic manuscripts in the Yale collections is one that served as a printer's copy. *The History of Florence* was written in Latin by the eminent scholar and book collector Poggio Bracciolini and translated into Italian by his son Jacopo. The manuscript is a handsome, though not a lavish, codex copied on paper by the scribe Niccolò Fonzio, who neatly foliated the leaves with red roman numerals in the upper margin. This text was later prepared and edited for printing. Square brackets appear together with symbols in the margin to mark text and page divisions, and the translator himself appears to have added corrections and annotations for the printer. Many of the manuscript leaves bear smudges of the typesetter's fingers.

The incunable edition, printed by Jacobus Rubeus in 1476, is similar to the manuscript. The typesetter has preserved both the broad format and the small details of the manuscript exemplar—headings, punctuation, and the line of capitals at the beginning of the preface. Yet there are differences as well. The scribe wrote the title and first line of text in alternating red and black rustic capitals, but the comparable portions of the printed page are in bold black square capitals. Printing in more than one color was a complex matter in the fifteenth century when the technology was still relatively new. What is perhaps most noticeable is the lack of an illuminated initial at the beginning of the printed text. The typesetter allotted the appropriate amount of space, but a decorative initial was never inserted. The letter *N* now appearing in the space is a much later pencil addition.

Although printing brought to a close the era of the handwritten text, the legacy of the medieval book lives on. It is the medieval book that transmitted and continues to transmit both religious and secular texts for centuries of readers and that helps historians to understand more fully the intellectual and personal lives of the people who owned them. The medieval book, from roll to codex, continues to speak eloquently of the culture that produced it.

Selected Readings

Alexander, J. J. G. *The Decorated Letter*. New York, 1978.

Backhouse, J. *The Illuminated Manuscript*. Oxford, 1979.

Bowman, A. K., and J. D. Thomas. *Vindolanda: the Latin Writing Tablets*, London, 1983, and *Vindolanda: the Latin Writing Tablets*, by A. K. Bowman and J. D. Thomas, with contributions by J. N. Adams and R. Tapper. Gloucester and London, 1983.

Bühler, C. F. *The Fifteenth Century Book: The Scribes, the Printers, the Decorators*. Philadelphia, 1960.

Cahn, W. *Romanesque Bible Illumination*. Ithaca, 1982.

Calkins, R. G. *Illuminated Books of the Middle Ages*. Ithaca, 1983.

De Hamel, C. F. R. *A History of Illuminated Manuscripts*. Boston, 1986.

Drogin, M. *Medieval Calligraphy: Its History and Technique*. Montclair, New Jersey, and London, 1980.

Hindman, S., and J. D. Farquhar. *Pen to Press: Illuminated Manuscripts and Printed Books in the First Century of Printing*. Exhibition Catalogue. Baltimore, 1977.

Hunter, D. *Papermaking: The History and Technique of an Ancient Craft*. 2d ed. New York, 1947; repr. New York, 1978.

Jackson, D. *The Story of Writing*. New York, 1981.

Lewis, N. *Papyrus in Classical Antiquity*. Oxford, 1974.

Miner, D. *The History of Bookbinding 525–1950: An Exhibition held at the Baltimore Museum of Art*. Baltimore, 1957.

Needham, P. *Twelve Centuries of Bookbindings, 400–1600*. Exhibition Catalogue. New York and London, 1979.

Pächt, O. *Book Illumination in the Middle Ages*. Oxford and New York, 1986.

——. *The Rise of Pictorial Narrative in Twelfth-Century England*. Oxford, 1962.

Reed, R. *Ancient Skins, Parchments and Leathers*. London and New York, 1972.

Reynolds, L. D., and N. G. Wilson. *Scribes and Scholars: A Guide to the Transmission of Greek and Latin Literature*. 2d ed. Oxford, 1974.

Roberts, C. H., and T. C. Skeat. *The Birth of the Codex*. Oxford, 1983.

Wieck, Roger S. *Time Sanctified. The Book of Hours in Medieval Art and Life*. New York, 1988.

Concordance

Beinecke Call Number	Catalogue Number	Beinecke Call Number	Catalogue Number	Beinecke Call Number	Catalogue Number
MS 3, no. 34	58	MS 401	11	Marston MS 52	34
MS 4	53	MS 402	13	Marston MS 67	92
MS 27	12	MS 404	82	Marston MS 77	16
MS 41	74	MS 407	5	Marston MS 141	59
MS 42	77	MS 408	101	Marston MS 152	18
MS 80	66	MS 410	83	Marston MS 155	31
MS 81	30	MS 413	28	Marston MS 157	29
MS 84	68	MS 414	38	Marston MS 180	91
MS 111	39	MS 417	44	Marston MS 213	76
MS 125	4	MS 425	48	Marston MS 242	90
MS 129	87	MS 427	89	Marston MS 247	57
MS 145	69	MS 428	43	Marston MS 262	67
MS 150	19	MS 433	79	Marston MS 268	63
MS 154	14	MS 436	45	Marston MS 287	65
MS 163	97	MS 438	47	Arabic MS 198	15
MS 171	100	MS 439	22	Arabic MS 321	50
MS 205	75	MS 446	98	Ethiopic MS 5	51
MS 207	94	MS 450	102	P.CtYBR inv. 8	1
MS 214	20	MS 454	99	P.CtYBR inv. 1253	21
MS 225	7	MS 481, Box 1, no. 1	25	P.CtYBR inv. 1788	3
MS 226	9	MS 481, Box 1, no. 2	26	P.CtYBR inv. 2125	24
MS 229	88	MS 481, Box 1, no. 3	27	P.CtYBR inv. 2753	2
MS 246	62	MS 481, Box 1, no. 5	71	Yale Law School MSSG/R 29/#32	56
MS 262	6	MS 482, Box 1, no. 3	72	Zi +4243	106
MS 275	8	MS 492	41		
MS 276	10	MS 493	49		
MS 281	84	MS 494	54		
MS 284	104	MS 516	70		
MS 286	32	MS 589	40	Other MSS Cited	Catalogue Number
MS 315	37	MS 604	78		
MS 321	105	MS 625	73	American Oriental Society MS Th/F84	52
MS 328	33	MS 648	96	Yale Medical Historical MS 12	93
MS 338	95	MS 653	17		
MS 382	35	MS 657	80		
MS 387	42	MS 660	85		
MS 390	46	MS 674	86		
MS 391	23	Marston MS 7	103		
MS 392	61	Marston MS 24	55		
MS 393	64	Marston MS 38	60		
MS 400	81	Marston MS 39	36		

Index

MEDIEVAL ACADEMY REPRINTS FOR TEACHING

Text Design: Greer Allen

Typesetting: Meriden-Stinehour Press

Printing: Eastern Press

Photography: Thor Moser

MART Cover Design: Elaine Cohen